MATHEMATICS

LAB MANUAL

CLASS-X

A Complete Lab Activity Book

Authors

Mr. Rohit Manglik
(N.I.T, Surathkal)

Mr. Mohit Tripathi
(M.Sc., B.Ed.)

Strictly according to the latest syllabus prescribed by

Central Board of Secondary Education (CBSE)

And

State Boards of Chhattisgarh, Haryana, Bihar, Jharkhand, Kerala, Mizoram,

Meghalaya, and other states following the CBSE curriculum

Title : Mathematics Lab Manual - X

Author Name : Mr. Rohit Manglik, Mr. Mohit Tripathi

Published By : EduGorilla Community Pvt. Ltd.

Publishers Address : 12/651, First Floor Opp. Arvindo Park, Near Jama Masjid, Indira Nagar, Lucknow, Uttar Pradesh - 226016, India

Copyright

ISBN: 9789355563453

Disclaimer

Compiled and Created by EduGorilla Book Experts

Printed by EduGorilla Community Pvt. Ltd.

PREFACE

With the NEP 2020 and expansion of research and knowledge has changed the face of education to a great extent. In the Modern times, education is not just constricted top the lecture method but also includes a practical knowledge of certain subjects. This way of education helps a student to grasp the basic concepts and principles. Thus, trying to break the stereotype that subjects like Mathematics, and Science means studying lengthy formulas, complex structures, and handling complicated instruments, we are trying to make education easy, fun, and enjoyable.

The new CBSE syllabus for Mathematics, which help in comprehension of concepts and try to develop the scientific attitude and basic laboratory skills desired at this level.

The present book Mathematics Lab Manual Class X has been written to meet the requirements of new curriculum in the practical work for class 10 following NEP 2020.

The purpose of this manual is not only to convey the approach of the laboratory courses but also to provide the students appropriate guidance required for carrying out the experiments in science laboratories. All the experiments in this manual have been given to conform a systematic format that includes Aim, Theory, Material Required, Procedure, Observation, Result, Precautions, Viva-Voce and Suggested Activities.

The Theory given with each experiment is a very special feature of this lab manual. It gives the complete understanding of each Concept/Term & Definition etc. so that students need not to refer their textbooks or any other book. Viva-Voce questions given with each experiment aims to test a student's understanding of the related experiment. To provide the student a basic idea of investigatory projects, some investigatory projects have been included as well.

SOME SPECIAL FEATURES

- Detailed and step-by-step procedure for each experiment.
- Viva-voce questions been designed to have grasp on the skill & knowledge required for an experiment
- Clearly labelled diagrams demonstrate the correct way of handling laboratory apparatus and pert the experiments methodically.

CONTENT

ACTIVITY 1

LINEAR EQUATIONS

OBJECTIVE

To verify the conditions for consistency of a system of linear equations in two variables by graphical representation.

LINEAR EQUATION

An equation of the form $ax + by + c = 0$, where a, b, c are real numbers, $a \neq 0, b \neq 0$ and x, y are variables; is called a linear equation in two variables.

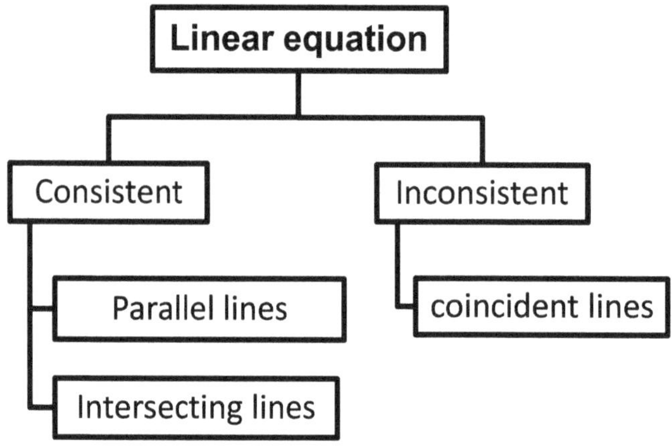

MATERIAL REQUIRED

Graph papers, fevicol, geometry box, cardboard.

THEORY

1. Plotting of points on a graph paper.
2. If the two lines intersect at a point, then the system is consistent and has a unique solution.
3. If the two lines are parallel to each other, then the system is inconsistent and has no solution.
4. If the two lines are coincident then the system is consistent and has infinitely many solutions.

PROCEDURE

Consider the three pairs of linear equations

1st pair: $2x - 5y + 4 = 0, 2x + y - 8 = 0$

2nd pair: $4x + 6y = 24, 2x + 3y = 6$

3rd pair: $x - 2y = 5, 3x - 6y = 15$

1. Take the 1st pair of linear equations in two variables, e.g., $2x - 5y + 4 = 0$, $2x + y - 8 = 0$.
2. Obtain a table of at least three such pairs (x, y) which satisfy the given equations.

For $2x - 5y + 4 = 0$

X	-2	0.5	3
Y	0	1	2

For $2x + y - 8 = 0$

X	2	3	4
Y	4	2	0

3. Plot the points of two equations on the graph paper as shown in fig.

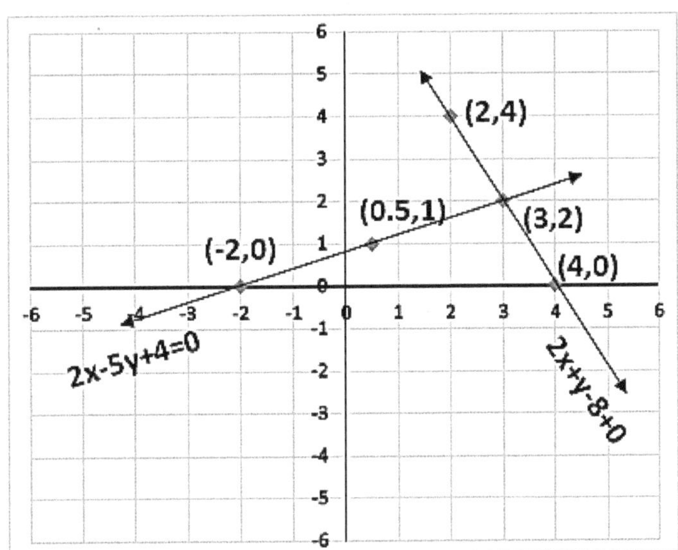

4. Observe whether the lines are intersecting, parallel or coincident. Write the values in the observation table.
Also check,

$$\frac{a_1}{a_2}, \frac{b_1}{b_2}, \frac{c_1}{c_2}$$

5. Take the second pair of linear equations in two variables.

For $4x + 6y = 24$

X	0	6	3
Y	4	0	2

For $2x + 3y = 6$

X	0	3	1.5
Y	2	0	1

6. Repeat steps 3 and 4.

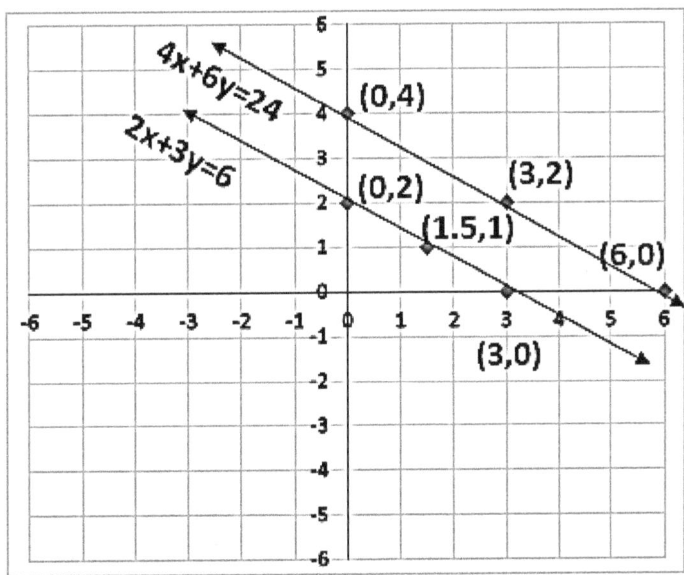

7. Take the third pair of linear equations in two variables, i.e., $x - 2y = 5$, $3x - 6y = 15$

For $x - 2y = 5$

X	1	5	0
Y	-2	0	-2.5

For $3x - 6y = 15$

X	0	1	5
Y	-2.5	-2	0

8. Repeat steps 3 and 4.
   Obtain the condition for two lines to be intersecting, parallel or coincident from the observation table by comparing the value of $\frac{a_1}{a_2}, \frac{b_1}{b_2}$ *and* $\frac{c_1}{c_2}$

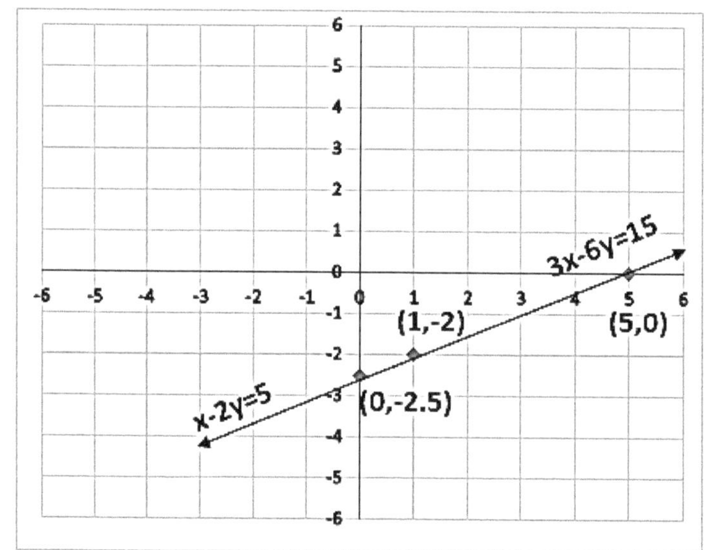

Observation table					
Pairs of lines	$\frac{a_1}{a_2}$	$\frac{b_1}{b_2}$	$\frac{c_1}{c_2}$	Compare the ratios and write conditions	Types of lines
1st pair					
2nd pair					
3rd pair					

OBSERVATION

Students will observe that

- for intersecting lines, $\frac{a_1}{a_2} \neq \frac{b_1}{b_2}$
- for parallel lines, $\frac{a_1}{a_2} = \frac{b_1}{b_2} \neq \frac{c_1}{c_2}$
- for coincident lines, $\frac{a_1}{a_2} = \frac{b_1}{b_2} = \frac{c_1}{c_2}$

RESULT

The conditions for consistency of a system of linear equations in two variables is verified.

LEARNING OUTCOME

Students will learn that some pairs of linear equations in two variables have a uniquesolution (intersecting lines), some have infinitely many solutions (coincident lines) and some have no solutions (parallel lines).

ACTIVITY TIME

Perform the same activity by drawing graphs of $x - y + 1 = 0$ and $3x + 2y - 12 = 0$. Showthat there is a unique solution. Also from the graph, calculate the area bounded by these linear equations and x-axis.

VIVA-VOCE

Question 1. What is the equation of a line parallel to the x-axis?
Answer: $y = a$, where a is any constant.

Question 2. What is the equation of a line parallel to the y-axis?
Answer: $x = b$, where b is any constant.

Question 3. If $x = 0$ and $y = 0$, where would the point lie on the graph?
Answer: At origin $(0,0)$

Question 4. If the graphical solutions of two linear equations of two lines intersect in a plane,then what type of solution do they have?
Answer: Unique solution.

Question 5. What does the graph of a linear equation represent?
Answer: A straight line.

Question 6. For what value of p does the pair of linear equations given below have unique solution?
$4x + 8 = 0, 2x + 2y + 2 = 0$
Answer: For a unique solution, $\frac{a_1}{a_2} \neq \frac{b_1}{b_2} \Rightarrow \frac{4}{2} \neq \frac{p}{2} \Rightarrow p \neq 4$

Question 7. If the graphical solutions of two linear equations of two lines are parallel to eachother in the plane, then what type of solution do they have?
Answer: No solution

Question 8. Is the pair of linear equations $2x + 3y - 9 = 0$ and $4x + 6y - 18 = 0$, consistent?
Answer: $\frac{a_1}{a_2} = \frac{b_1}{b_2} = \frac{c_1}{c_2} = \frac{1}{2}$
Here given system of equations is consistent and has infinitely many solutions.

MULTIPLE CHOICE QUESTION

Question 1.
Is $x = -1, y = 5$ a solution of the equation $4x + 3y = 11$?
(a) yes
(b) no
(c) can't say
(d) none of these

Question 2.
Equations $5x + 2y = 16$ and $7x - 4y = 2$ have:
(a) no solution
(b) a unique solution
(c) infinitely many solutions
(d) none of these

Question 3.
Equations $-3x + 4y = 5$ and $\frac{9}{2}x - 6y = \frac{15}{2}$
(a) a unique solution
(b) infinitely many solutions
(c) no solution
(d) none of these

Question 4.
Equations $-3x + 4y = 5$ and $\frac{9}{2}x - 6y + \frac{15}{2} = 0$ have:
(a) many solutions
(b) a unique solution
(c) no solution
(d) none of these

Question 5.

Condition for system of linear equations $ax + by = c;\ lx + my = n$ to have a uniquesolution is:

(a) $\mathrm{am} \neq \mathrm{bl}$

(b) $\mathrm{am} = \mathrm{bl}$

(c) $\frac{a}{l} = \frac{b}{m} = \frac{c}{n}$

(d) none of these

Question 6.

When l_1 and $l_2$are parallel lines, then the graphical solution of a system of linear equations has

(a) many solutions

(b) no solution

(c) a unique solution

(d) none of these

Question 7.

When lines $l_1$and l_2 are coincident, then the graphical solution of the system of linear equations has

(a) infinitely many solutions

(b) a unique solution

(c) no solution

(d) parallel lines

Question 8.

Values of x and y for the pair of linear equations $x + y = 14$ and $x - y = 4$ are respectively

(a) 9 and 5

(b) 5 and 9

(c) 5 and 5

(d) 9 and 9

Question 9.

The difference between two numbers is 26 and one number are three times the other. The numbers are

(a) 39 and 12

(b) 39 and 13

(c) 38 and 13

(d) 13 and 13

Question 10.

In a cyclic quadrilateral BACD, $\angle A = (2x-4)°$, $\angle B = (y+5)°$, $\angle C = (2y+10)°$ and $\angle D = (4x-2)°$. Find four angles.

(a) $\angle A = 58°, \angle B = 60°, \angle C = 120°, \angle D = 122°$

(b) $\angle A = 65°, \angle B = 55°, \angle C = 115°, \angle D = 125°$

(c) $\angle A = 70°, \angle B = 110°, \angle C = 55°, \angle D = 125°$

(d) $\angle A = 65°, \angle B = 55°, \angle C = 110°, \angle D = 127°$

Answer Key

1.(a)	2.(b)	3.(c)	4.(a)	5.(a)	6.(b)	7.(a)	8.(a)	9.(b)	10.(a)

ACTIVITY 2

ARITHMATIC PROGRESSION

OBJECTIVE

To verify that the given sequence is an arithmetic progression by paper cutting and pasting method.

ARITHMETIC PROGRESSION

A sequence is known as an arithmetic progression (sequence) if the difference between the term and its predecessor always remains constant.

MATERIAL REQUIRED

Coloured papers, a pair of scissors, fevicol, geometry box, sketch pens, drawing sheets.

THEORY

Understanding the concept of an arithmetic progression.

PROCEDURE

1. Take a given sequence of numbers that says A_1, A_2, A_3, ...
2. Cut a rectangular strip from the coloured paper of width 1 cm and length A cm.
3. Repeat the procedure by cutting rectangular strips of same width 1 cm and lengths A_1,... A_3...cm.
4. Take a graph paper and paste these rectangular strips adjacent to each other in order on graph paper.

[A] Consider a sequence 1, 4, 7, 10, 13.

1. Take different colour strips of lengths 1 cm, 4 cm, 7 cm, 10 cm, 13 cm and all of the same width 1 cm (say).
2. Arrange and paste these strips in order on a graph paper as shown in fig. (i)

[B] Consider a sequence 1, 4, 8, 10, 11.

1. Take different colour strips of lengths 1 cm, 4 cm, 8 cm, 10 cm, 11cm and all of the same width 1 cm (say).
2. Arrange and paste these strips in order on a graph paper as shown in fig. (ii)

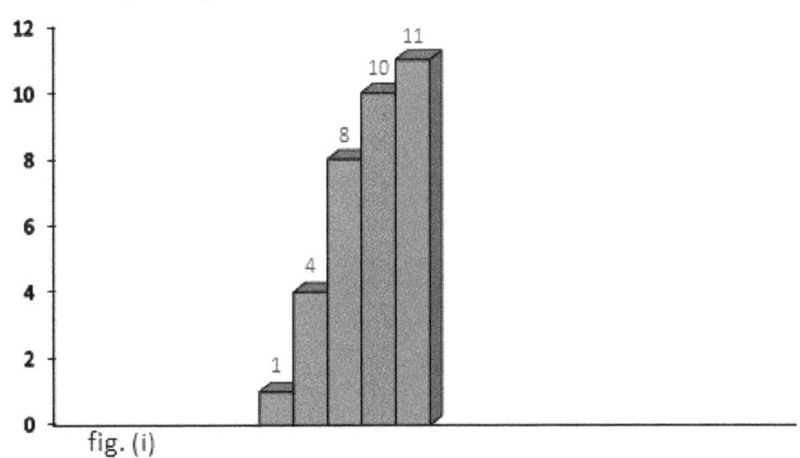

fig. (i)

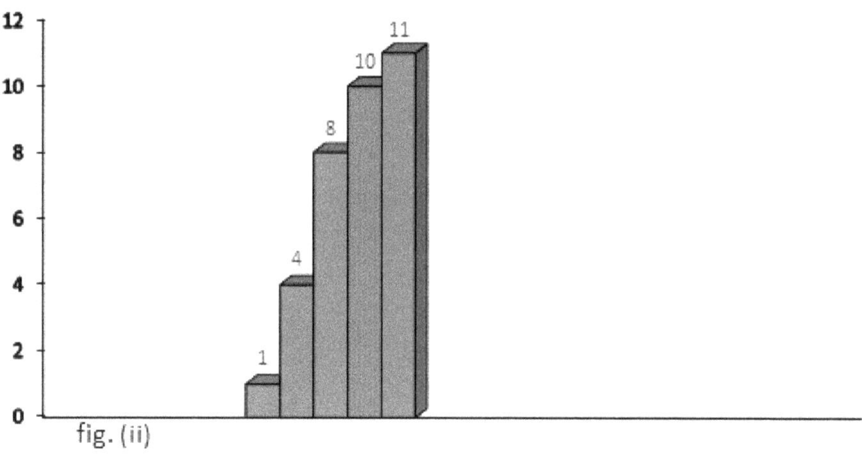

fig. (ii)

OBSERVATION

We observe from fig(i) that the adjoining strips have a common difference in heights i.e., 3 cm and a ladder is formed in which the adjoining steps are constant. Hence it isan arithmetic progression. In fig (ii) the adjoining strips don't have a common difference in heights and thus the adjoining steps of the ladder are not constant. Hence it is not an arithmetic progression.

	$fig(i)$	$fig.(ii)$
Observation	There is a common difference in heights i.e., $3\ \mathrm{cm}$	Don't have a common difference in heights
Result	It is an AP.	Not an AP.

RESULT

Sequence **[A]** is an AP because the common difference between the term and its predecessor remains constant.

Sequence **[B]** is not an AP because the common difference between the term and its predecessor does not remain constant.

LEARNING OUTCOME

Students will learn the meaning of an arithmetic progression by relating it to anactivity that involves visualization.

ACTIVITY TIME

Verify experimentally whether the following sequences are AP or not.

(i) 2, 4, 6, 8, 10
(ii) 3, 5, 6, 7, 11
(iii) 1, 5, 9, 13, 17
(iv) 4, 7, 9, 10, 12

ACTIVITY AT A GLANCE

- Take Numbers
- Cut rctangular strips of lenghts of numbers
- Paste the strips adjacent to each other.
- Observe the common difference in heights
- **1. If it is same then it is an AP.**
- **2.If it is not same then it is not an AP.**

VIVA-VOCE

Question 1. What is the common difference for an AP?
Answer: The difference between a term and its predecessor is called the common difference in an AP.

Question 2. Is the sequence of odd natural numbers an AP?
Answer: Yes.

Question 3. What does $I_n - I_{n-1}$ represent for an AP, where I_n and I_{n-1} represent consecutive terms of an AP?
Answer: Common difference.

Question 4. Are the numbers $2, 4, 7, 10, 11$ in AP?
Answer: No

Question 5. What is the common difference of a sequence of multiples of 4?
Answer:4

Question 6. What is the formula for the nth term of an AP?
Answer: $\mathrm{Tn} = \mathrm{a} + (\mathrm{n} - 1)$ where a- first term. d- the common difference a place of the term.

Question 7. Find next two terms of $-11,-8,-5,-2$.
Answer: 1, 4

Question 8. Find k, so that 15, k, -1 are in an AP.
Answer: k =7

MULTIPLE CHOICE QUESTION

Question 1.
The nth term of an AP is
(a) $\mathrm{a} + (\mathrm{n} - 1)\mathrm{d}$
(b) $\mathrm{a} - (\mathrm{n} - 1)\mathrm{d}$
(c) $\mathrm{a} - (\mathrm{n} + 1)\mathrm{d}$
(d) none of these

Question 2.
20th term of the series $4, 7, 10, \ldots \ldots$ is
(a) 51
(b) 59
(c) 61
(d) 62

Question 3.

Which sequence forms an AP?

(a) $3, 3+\sqrt{2}, 3+2\sqrt{2}$

(b) $3, 3+\sqrt{2}, 3 + 2$

(c) $3, 3+\sqrt{2}, 3-2\sqrt{2}$

(d) none of these

Question 4.

If $a = 7$ and $d = 3$, then a_8

(a) 27

(b) 26

(c) 25

(d) 28

Question 5.

The 30 term of the AP 10,7,4 is

(a) 97

(b) 77

(c) −77

(d) −87

Question 6.

Find the missing terms of an AP 5,.......,$9\frac{1}{2}$

(a) $8, 9\frac{1}{2}$

(b) $6, 8$

(c) $6, 8\frac{1}{2}$

(d) none of these

Question 7.

Which term of the AP 3,8,13,18, ... is 78?

(a) 16th term

(b) 17th term

(c) 18th term

(d) 19th term

Question 8.

If d= 3, n = 18 and $a_n = -5$, then $a =$

(a) 44

(b) 45

(c) 46

(d) none of these

Question 9.

If the nth term of an AP is $7 - 4n$, the common difference d is

(a) 3

(b) −3

(c) −4

(d) 4

Question 10.

How many three-digit numbers are divisible by 7?

(a) 121

(b) 125

(c) 127

(d) 128

Question 11:

Find the first four terms of the AP whose first term is -1 and the common difference is $\frac{1}{2}$

(a) $-1, \frac{-1}{2}, 0, \frac{1}{2}$

(b) $1, \frac{-1}{2}, 0, \frac{1}{2}$

(c) $1, \frac{-1}{2}, 1, \frac{1}{2}$

(d) None of these

Answer Key

1.(a)	2.(c)	3.(a)	4.(d)	5.(c)	6.(a)	7.(a)	8.(c)	9.(c)	10.(d)
11.(a)									

ACTIVITY 3

ARITHMATIC PROGRESSION II

OBJECTIVE

To verify that the sum of first n natural numbers is $\frac{n(n+1)}{2}$ by graphical method.
The product of two polynomials say A and B represents a rectangle of sides A and B.Thus n(n+1) represents a rectangle of sides n and (n + 1).

MATERIAL REQUIRED

Graph papers, white chart paper, coloured pens, geometry box.

THEORY

1. Concept of natural numbers.
2. Area of squares and rectangles.

PROCEDURE

Let us consider the sum of first n natural numbers $1 + 2 + 3 + 4 + \cdots n$ (say $n = 10$).

1. Take a graph paper and paste it on white chart paper.
2. Mark the rectangles $1, 2, 3, n, (n + 1)$ along the vertical line and $1,2,3, n$ along the horizontal line.
3. Colour the rectangular strips of length 1 cm, 2 cm, 3 cm, n cm each of width 1 cm.
4. Complete the rectangle with sides n and $n + 1$. Name this rectangle as PQRS. Mark dot in each square as shown in fig.

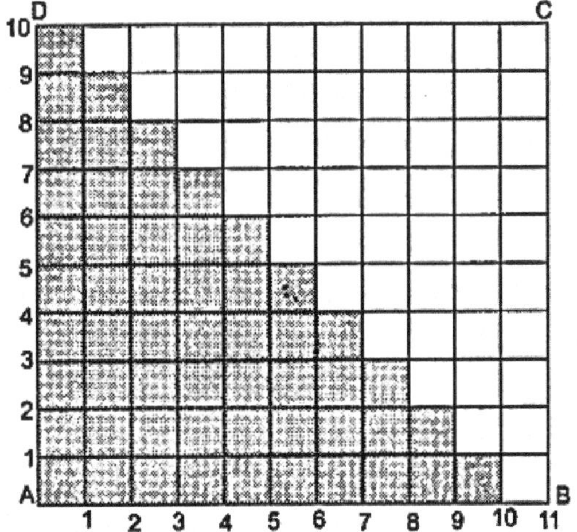

5. Count the coloured squares and the total number of squares in rectangle PQRS.

OBSERVATION

We observe, number of shaded squares $= \frac{1}{2} \times$ total no. of squares
No. of shaded squares $= 1 + 2 + 3 + \cdots + n$
Total squares = Area of rectangle $= n\,(n + 1)$
Therefore $1 + 2 + 3 + \cdots n = \frac{1}{2}\, n(n + 1)$

MATHEMATICALLY

Area of rectangle PQRS $= 10 \times 11$
Area of shaded region $= \frac{1}{2} \times 10 \times 11 = 55$ .... (i)

Also, area of shaded region $= (1 \times 1) + (2 \times 1) + (3 \times 1) + \cdots (10 \times 1)$
$= 1 + 2 + 3 + \cdots 10 = 55$.....................**(ii)**

From (i) and (ii),

$$1 + 2 + 3 + \ldots + 10 = \frac{1}{2} \times 10 \times 11 = 55$$

Verified that $1 + 2 + 3 + \ldots 10 = \frac{1}{2} \times 10 \times (10 + 1)$ by graphical method.

RESULT

It is verified graphically that $1 + 2 + 3 + \cdots + n = \frac{1}{2}n(n + 1)$ or sum of first n natural numbers $= \frac{1}{2}n(n + 1)$.

LEARNING OUTCOME

Students will develop a geometrical intuition of the formula for the sum of natural numbers starting from one.

ACTIVITY TIME

1. Find the sum of the first 100 natural numbers.
2. Find the sum of the first 1000 natural numbers.
3. Evaluate $10 + 11 + 12 + \cdots 25$.

VIVA-VOCE

Question 1. Are all natural numbers whole numbers?
Answer: Yes

Question 2. Are all whole numbers natural numbers?
Answer: Except zero, all whole numbers are natural numbers.

Question 3. Write down an AP having the sum of the first 7 terms as zero.
Answer: $-3, -2, -1, 0, 1, 2, 3$.

Question 4. Find the common difference of an arithmetic progression of the first 20 naturalnumbers.
Answer: 1

Question 5. What is the formula for the sum of n terms of an AP?
Answer: $Sn = \frac{n}{2}[2a + (n - 1)d]$

Question 6. What is the formula for the sum of n terms of an AP whose common difference is not given?
[First term a and last term l known]
Answer: $Sn = \frac{n}{2}[a + l]$, where l represents the last term.

Question 7. If $S_n = 3n^2 + 2n$, find the first term.
Answer: 5

Question 8. What is the arithmetic mean of 4 and 8?
Answer: 6

Question 9. What is the sum of the first 10 natural numbers?
Answer:55

MULTIPLE CHOICE QUESTION

Question 1.
The Sum of the first n^{th} terms of an AP is
(a) $\frac{n}{2}[2a + (n - 1)d]$
(b) $\frac{n}{2}2n[a + (n - 1)d]$
(c) $\frac{n}{2}[2a - (n - 1)d]$
(d) $\frac{n}{2}[2a - (n + 1)d]$

Question 2.
The Sum of first n positive integers is
(a) $\frac{n(n-1)}{2}$
(b) $\frac{2n(n+1)}{2}$
(c) $\frac{n(n+1)}{2}$
(d) none of these

Question 3.
The sum of $0.70 + 0.71 + 0.72 + \ldots .to\ 50$ terms is
(a) 4.725
(b) 47.25
(c) 472.5
(d) none of these

Question 4.
If $a_n = 3 + 4n$ is n^{th} the term of an AP, then S_{15} is
(a) 525
(b) 325
(c) 425
(d) none of these

Question 5.
The Sum of all odd numbers between 0 and 50 is
(a) 623
(b) 627
(c) 624
(d) 625

Question 6.
Sum of $-37, -33, -29, \ldots\ to\ 12$ terms is
(a) -180
(b) 180
(c) 108
(d) -108

Question 7.
In an AP, given that $a_{12} = 37$ and d= 3. Find S_{12}.
(a) 246
(b) 642
(c) 264
(d) 624

Question 8.
In an AP, if $a = 8, a_n = 62$ and $S_n = 210$, then n is
(a) 4
(b) 6
(c) 5
(d) 7

Question 9.
The sum of the first 40 positive integers divisible by 6 is
(a) 4092
(b) 4029
(c) 4920
(d) 4290

Question 10.
The sum of the first 15 multiples of 8 is
(a) 690
(b) 609
(c) 906
(d) 960

Answer Key

1.(a)	2.(c)	3.(b)	4.(a)	5.(d)	6.(a)	7.(a)	8.(b)	9.(c)	10.(d)

ACTIVITY 4 SUM OF ODD NATURAL NUMBERS

OBJECTIVE

To verify that the sum of first n odd natural numbers, $1 + 3 + 5 + \cdots + (2n - 1) = n$ by paper activity.

MATERIAL REQUIRED

Squared papers, sketch pens, pencil, a pair of scissors, geometry box, fevicol, white drawing sheets

THEORY

1. Natural numbers (i.e., counting numbers e.g., $1, 2, 3, 4, \ldots$)
2. Odd natural numbers (Natural numbers which are not divisible by 2 i.e. $1, 3, 5, \ldots$)
3. Even natural numbers (Natural numbers which are divisible by 2 i.e. $2, 4, 6,$)
4. Formula to find the nth term of an AP i.e., $a_n = a + (n - 1)d$
   where a–first term, d-common difference, n - no. of terms
5. For odd natural numbers $1, 3, 5, \ldots\ldots n^{th}$ term is
   $a_n = 1 + (n - 1).2 = (2n - 1)$
6. Area of squares.

PROCEDURE

1. Take a squared chart paper of size $n\ units \times n\ units$ (take $n - 9$).

2. Paste it on a white sheet.
3. Colour the internal squares with different 9 colours as shown in fig.

P	W	R	O	Y	G	B	I	V
P	W	R	O	Y	G	B	I	I
P	W	R	O	Y	G	B	B	B
P	W	R	O	Y	G	G	G	G
P	W	R	O	Y	Y	Y	Y	Y
P	W	R	O	O	O	O	O	O
P	W	R	R	R	R	R	R	R
P	W	W	W	W	W	W	W	W
P	P	P	P	P	P	P	P	P

V-Violet
I-Indigo
B-Blue
G-Green
Y-Yellow
O-Orange
R-Red
W-White
P-Pink

4. Put a black dot on each of the internal coloured squares as shown in fig.

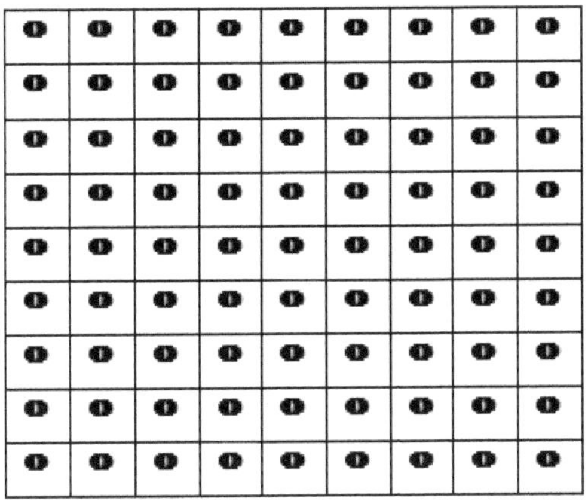

OBSERVATION

S.No	No. of shaded squares	No. of dots	Square	In term of
1.	Violet colour =1	1	(1×1) squares	1^2
2.	Violet + Indigo =1+3	4	(2×2) squares	2^2
3.	Violet + Indigo + Blue =1+3+5	9	(3×3) squares	3^2
4.	Violet+Indigo+Blue+Green = 1+3+5+7	16	(4×4) squares	4^2
5.	V+I+ B+ G+Y = 1+3+5+7+9	25	(5×5) squares	5^2
.				
.				
9	V+I+B+G+Y+O+R +W+P =1+3+5+7+9+13 +15+17	81	(9×9) squares	9^2
.				
.				
n	1+3+5+···+ up to n terms	$n \times n$	$(n \times n)$ squares	n^2

Proceeding in the same way and generalising the result on the above table, we can say that the number of dots in $n \times n$ squares $= n^2$.

RESULT

The sum of first n odd natural numbers is n i.e., $1 + 3 + 5 + 7 + \cdots (2n - 1) = n$

LEARNING OUTCOME

Through this activity, students can find that the sum of first n odd natural numbers n^2i.e., $\sum(2n - 1) = n^2$

ACTIVITY TIME

1. Find out the sum of the first fifteen odd natural numbers with the help of the above activity and verify the result using the formula $\sum(2n - 1) = n^2$
2. Find the sum of $(11 + 13 + \ldots + 21)$ using the result of this activity.

VIVA-VOCE

Question 1. What is the sum of first n natural numbers?

Answer: $S_n = \frac{n(n+1)}{2}$

Question 2. Give the formula for the sum of first $(n+1)$ natural numbers.

Answer: $S_{n+1} = \frac{(n+2)(n+1)}{2}$

Question 3: What is the sum of first n multiples of 5?

Answer: $\frac{5 \times n(n+1)}{2}$

Question 4. What is the sum of $2 + 6 + 10 + 14 + 18 + \cdots$ 10 terms?

Answer: 200

[**Hint:**$2[1 + 3 + 5 + \cdots + 10 \text{ terms}] = 2 \times 10^2 = 200$]

Question 5. What is the nth term of $1 + 3 + 5$?

Answer: $a_n = (2n - 1)$

Question 6. What is the nth term of $2 + 4 + 6$?

Answer: $a_n = 2n$

Question 7. Give the formula for the sum to n terms of an AP.

Answer: $S_n = \frac{n}{2}[2a + (n-1)d]$

Question 8. Define odd numbers and which is the first odd natural number.

Answer: Numbers that are not divisible by 2 are known as odd numbers. 1 is the first oddnatural number.

MULTIPLE CHOICE QUESTION

Question 1.

Find n for $\frac{n(n+1)}{2}$ =55

(a) -11
(b) 10
(c) 11
(d) None of these

Question 2.

Using, $\frac{n(n+1)}{2}$ evaluate 1 + 3 + 5 + 7 + 9.

(a) 24
(b) 23
(c) 25
(d) 26

Question 3.

If the nth term of an AP is (2n + 1), find the sum of the first n^{th} terms of the AP.

(a) $n(n+2)$
(b) $n(n-2)$
(c) $(n^2 - 2)$
(d) None of these

Question 4.

For AP 5 + 4 + 3 + 2 + 1+ 0 + (-1) + what should be its last term so that sum of all terms is zero?

(a) -4
(b) -7
(c) -5
(d) None of these

Question 5.

In AP $16 + 12 + 8 + 4 + 0 + (-4) + (-8) + (-12) + S_7$ is

(a) 28
(b) 16
(c) 20
(d) None of these

Question 6:

Common difference of an AP $\sqrt{2}$, $\sqrt{8}, \sqrt{18}, \sqrt{32}$ is

(a) $\sqrt{3}$ (c) $2\sqrt{3}$
(b) $\sqrt{2}$ (d) 4

Question 7.
First-term of an AP is p, and its common difference is q then its 10th term is
(a) $9p + q$
(b) $p - 9q$
(c) $p + 9q$
(d) None of these

Question 8.
The sum of the first n positive integer S_n is
(a) $S_n = \frac{n(n-1)}{2}$
(b) $S_n = \frac{n(n+1)}{2}$
(c) $S_n = \frac{n}{2}[2a + (n-1)d]$
(d) $T_n = a + (n-1)d$

Question 9.
20th term of the series $4, 7, 10, \dots \dots$ is
(a) 61
(b)60
(c) 59
(d) None of these

Question 10.
Choose the correct option: First four terms of the AP whose first term is $-1$and the common difference is $\frac{1}{2}$
(a) $1, -\frac{1}{2}, \frac{1}{2}, 0$
(b) $1, 0, -\frac{1}{2}, \frac{1}{2}$
(c) $1, -\frac{1}{2}, 0, \frac{1}{2}$
(d) $0, -\frac{1}{2}, \frac{1}{2}, 1$

Answer Key

1.(b)	2.(c)	3.(a)	4.(c)	5.(a)	6.(b)	7.(c)	8.(b)	9.(a)	10.(c)

ACTIVITY 5 BASIC PROPORTIONALITY THEOREM FOR A TRIANGLE

OBJECTIVE

To verify the basic proportionality theorem by using parallel lines board, triangle cutouts.

BASIC PROPORTIONALITY THEOREM

If a line is drawn parallel to one side of a triangle, to intersect the other two sides at distinct points, the other two sides are divided in the same ratio.

MATERIAL REQUIRED

White chart paper, coloured papers, geometry box, sketch pens, fevicol, a pair of scissors, ruled paper sheet (or Parallel line board).

THEORY

1. Statement of Basic Proportionality theorem.
2. Drawing a line parallel to a given line which passes through a givenpoint.

PROCEDURE

1. Cut an acute-angled triangle say ABC from coloured paper.
2. Paste the ΔABC on the ruled sheet such that the base of the trianglecoincides with the ruled line.

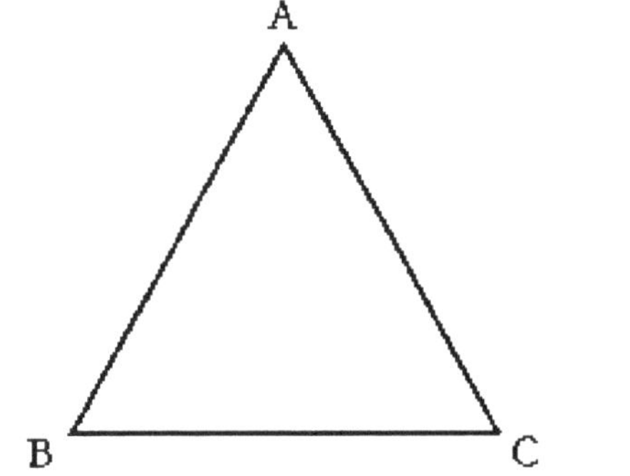

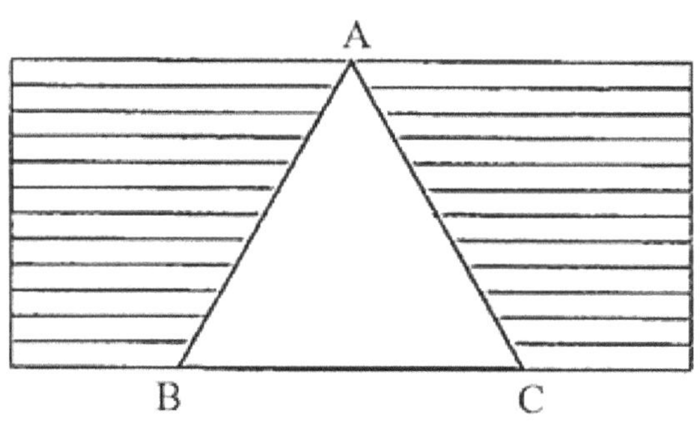

3. Mark two points P and Q on AB and AC such that PQ || BC.

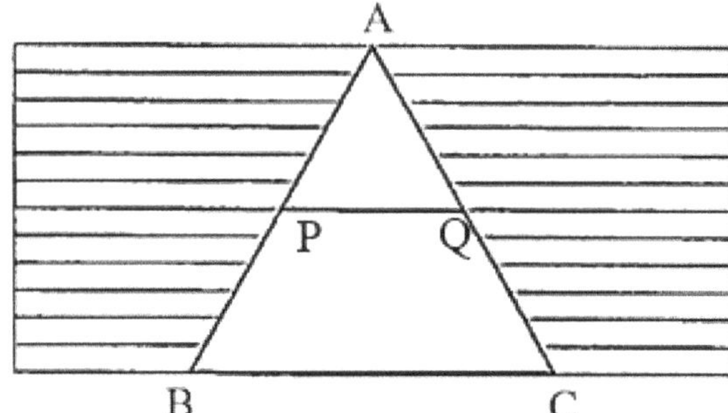

4. Using a ruler measure the length of AP, PB, AQ and QC.
5. Repeat the same for the right-angled triangle and obtuse-angled triangle.
6. Now complete the following observation table.

OBSERVATION

Triangle ABC	Length of the segment				$\frac{AP}{PB}$	$\frac{AQ}{QC}$	Equal / Not equal
	AP	PB	AQ	QC			
Acute							
Obtuse							
Right							

RESULT

In each set of triangles, we verified that $\frac{AP}{PB} = \frac{AQ}{QC}$

LEARNING OUTCOME

Students will observe that in all three triangles the Basic Proportionality theoremis verified.

ACTIVITY TIME

1. Find x if DE || BC.

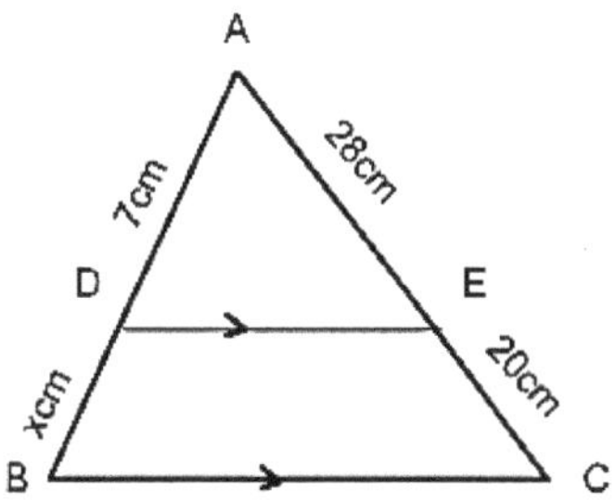

2. Is PQ || AB?

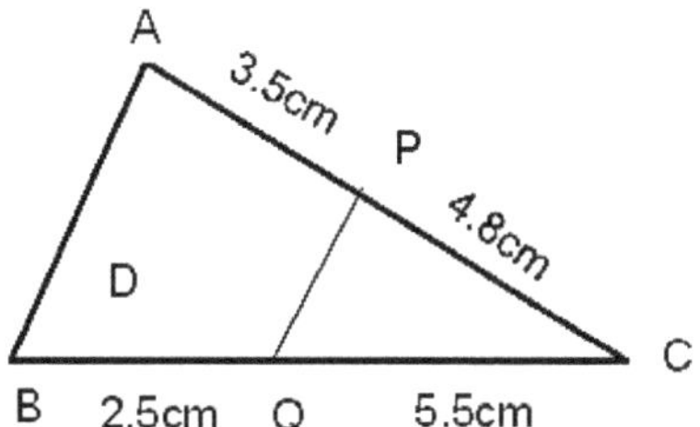

3. Find x if PQ || BC

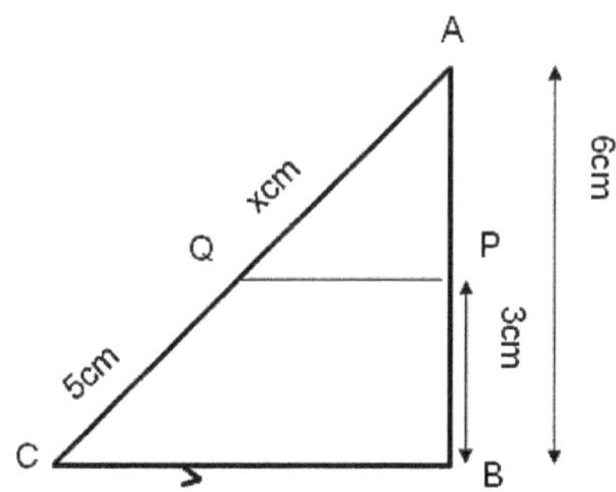

VIVA-VOCE

Question 1. Is there any other name for B.P.T. (Basic Proportionality Theorem)?
Answer: Yes, Thales Theorem.

Question 2. Name the mathematician who gave B.P.T.
Answer: Greek mathematician Thales

Question 3. What is the statement of B.P.T.?
Answer: If a line is drawn parallel to one side of a triangle to intersect the other two sides atdistinct points, the other two sides are divided in the same ratio.

Question 4. What is the converse of B.P.T.?
Answer: If a line divides any two sides of a triangle in the same ratio, the line is parallel to thethird side of the triangle.

Question 5. Is the B.P.T. applicable for a scalene triangle?
Answer: Yes

Question 6. Can we prove the Mid-point theorem by using B.P.T.?
Answer: Yes

Question 7. Give two different examples of pairs of similar figures.
Answer: Pair of squares, pair of circles

Question 8. What are the conditions for two polygons of the same number of sides to be similar?
Answer: (a) Their corresponding angles are equal.
(b) Their corresponding sides are proportional.

MULTIPLE CHOICE QUESTION

Question 1.
In the given fig., AB || DE and BD || EF. Find the correct relation.

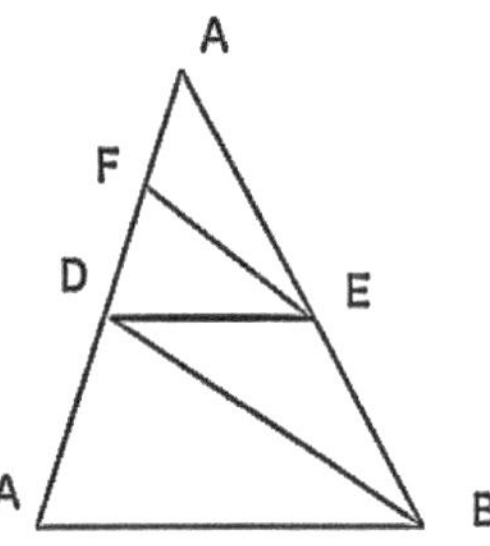

(a) $DC^2 = CF \times AC$
(b) $CF^2 = DC \times AC$
(c) $AC^2 = DC \times CF$
(d) None of these

Question 2.
In ΔABC, if DE || BC, AD = 3.2, DB = 1.6, AE = x and EC = 2.1, then x is
(a) 4.2
(b) 3.2
(c) 1.6
(d) 4.8

Question 3.
In the given fig., LM || QR. Find LQ

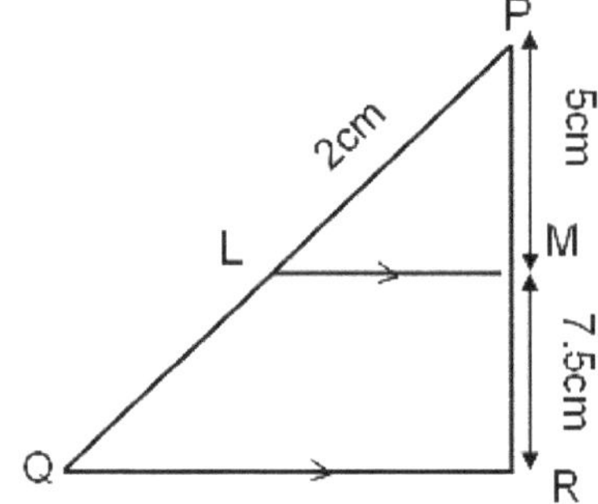

(a) 3.1 cm
(b) 2.5 cm
(c) 3 cm
(d) None of these

Question 4.
$\triangle ABC \sim \triangle PQR$, $\angle B = 50°$ and $\angle C = 70°$ then $\angle P$ is equal to
(a) 50°
(b) 60°
(c) 40°
(d) 70°

Question 5.
In the given fig., DE || BC. If $\frac{AE}{AC} = \frac{2}{5}$ and AB = 15 cm, find AD.

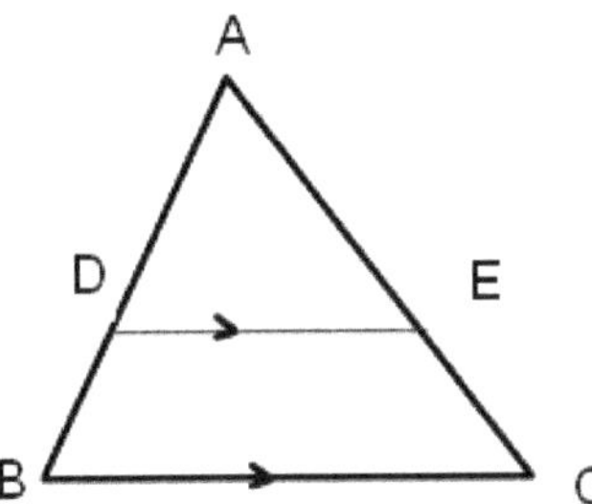

(a) 6 cm
(b) 5 cm
(c) 4 cm
(d) 7 cm

Question 6.
If LM || CB and LN || CD, then choose the correct answer

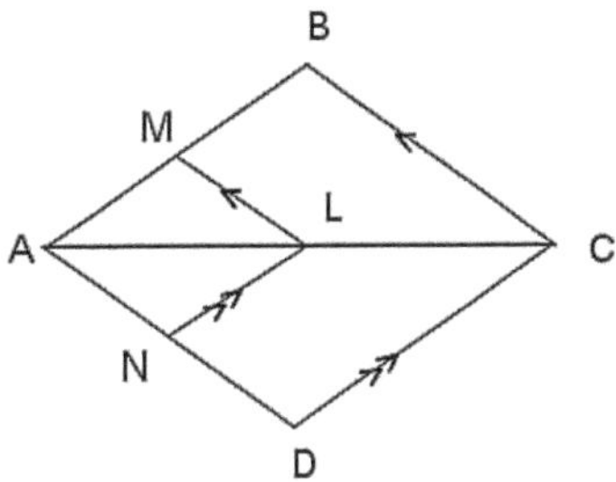

(a) $\frac{AM}{AB} = \frac{AN}{AD}$
(b) $\frac{AM}{AB} = \frac{AN}{AD}$
(c) $\frac{AM}{AB} \neq \frac{AN}{AD}$
(d) $\frac{AB}{AM} = \frac{AN}{AD}$

Question 7.
What value of p will make ST || QR in the given fig.?

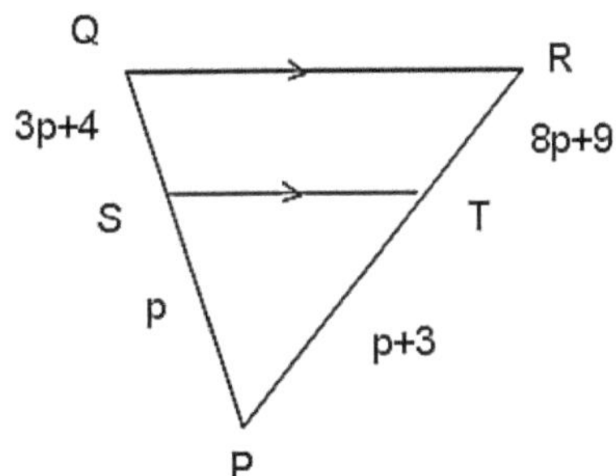

(a) 2
(b) 3
(c) 5
(d) None of these

Question 8.
In the given figure, DE || OQ and DF || OR, then which is the correct relation?

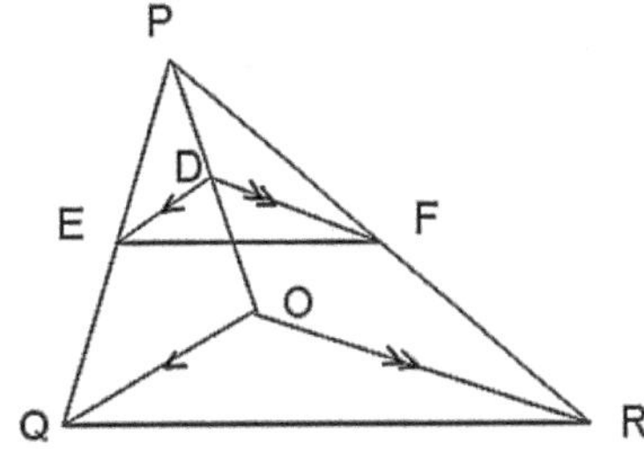

(a) $EF = \frac{1}{2}QR$
(b) $EF \neq QR$
(c) $EF = QR$
(d) $EF \parallel QR$

Question 9.
Find $x$if DC || AB.

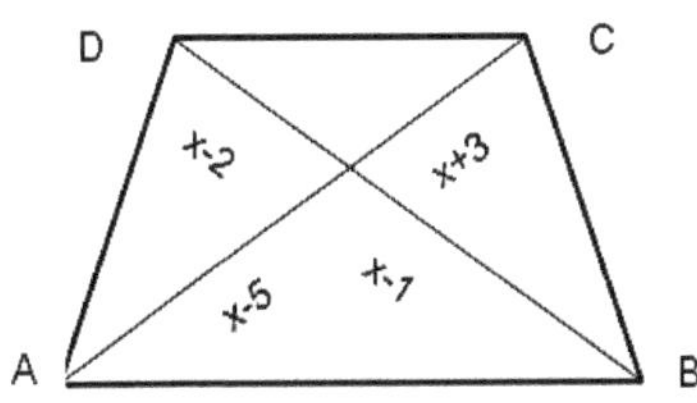

(a) 7
(b) 3
(c) 5
(d) None of these

Question 10.
In the given figure DE || BC, then EC is

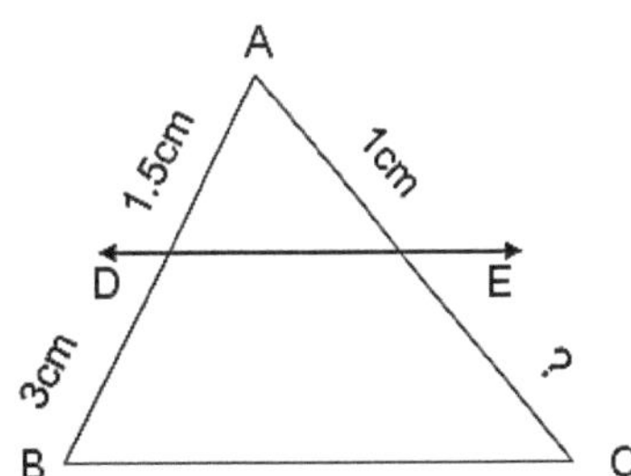

(a) 2 cm
(b) 1.5 cm
(c) 1 cm
(d) 3 cm

Question 11.

In the given figure ABC and AMP are two right triangles, right-angled at B and Mrespectively. Then tick the correct answer.

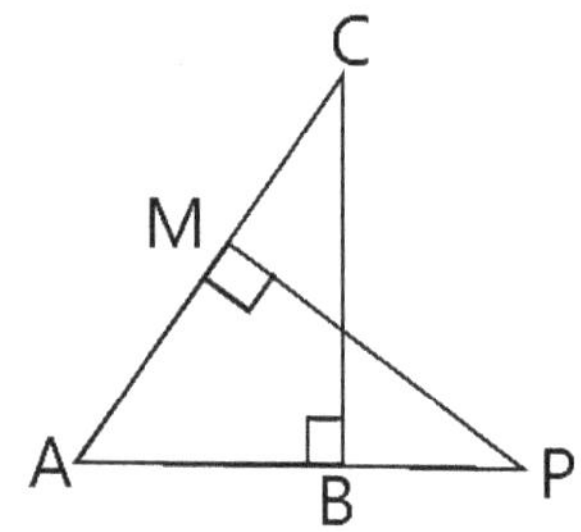

(a) $\frac{CA}{PA} = \frac{BC}{MP}$

(b) $\frac{CA}{PA} \neq \frac{BC}{MP}$

(c) $\frac{CA}{PA} = \frac{MP}{BC}$

(d) $\frac{CA}{PA} \neq \frac{MP}{BC}$

Answer Key

1.(a)	2.(c)	3.(a)	4.(a)	5.(d)	6.(a)	7.(a)	8.(d)	9.(a)	10.(a)
11.(a)									

ACTIVITY 6

PYHTAGORAS THEOREM

OBJECTIVE

To verify Pythagoras theorem by performing an activity.

The area of the square constructed on the hypotenuse of a right-angled triangle isequal to the sum of the areas of squares constructed on the other two sides of a right-angled triangle.

MATERIAL REQUIRED

Coloured papers, pair of scissors, fevicol, geometry box, sketch pens, light coloured square sheet.

THEORY

1. In a right-angled triangle, the square of the hypotenuse is equal to the sumof squares on the other two sides.
2. Concept of a right-angled triangle.
3. Area of square = $(\text{side})^2$
4. Construction of perpendicular lines.

PROCEDURE

1. Take a coloured paper, draw and cut a right-angled triangle ACB right- angled at C, of sides 3 cm, 4 cm and 5 cm as shown in fig.

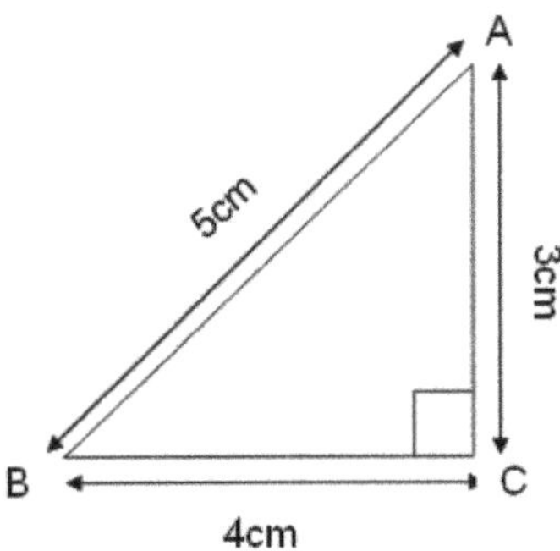

2. Paste this triangle on the white sheet of paper.
3. Draw squares on each side of the triangle on side AB, BC and AC andname them accordingly as shown in fig.

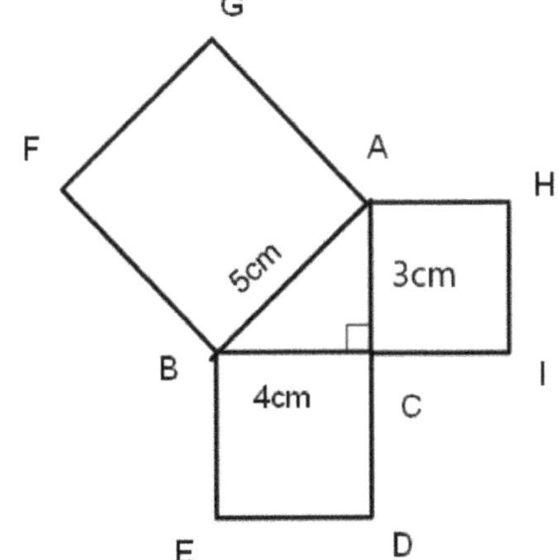

4. Extend the sides FB and GA of the square ABFG which meets ED at Pand CI at Q

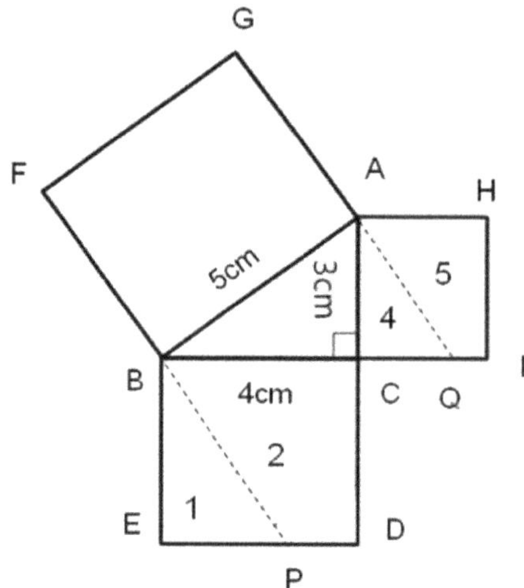

respectively, as shown in fig.

5. Draw perpendicular RP on BP which meets CD at R. Mark the parts 1, 2,3, 4 and 5 of the squares BCDE and ACIH and colour them with five different colours as shown in fig.

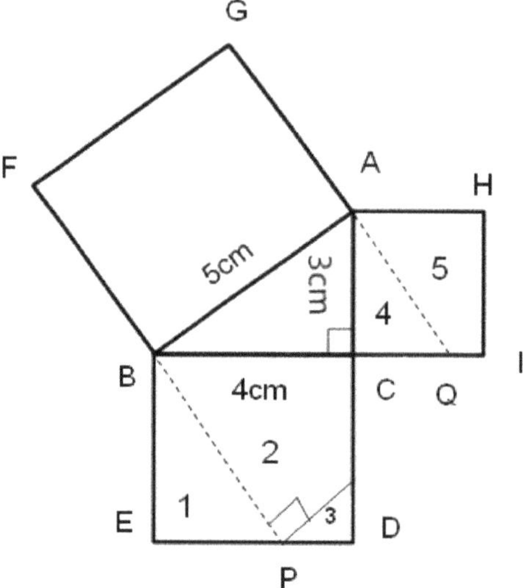

6. Cut the pieces 1, 2, 3, 4 and 5 from the squares BCDE and ACIH andplace the pieces on the square ABFG as shown in fig.

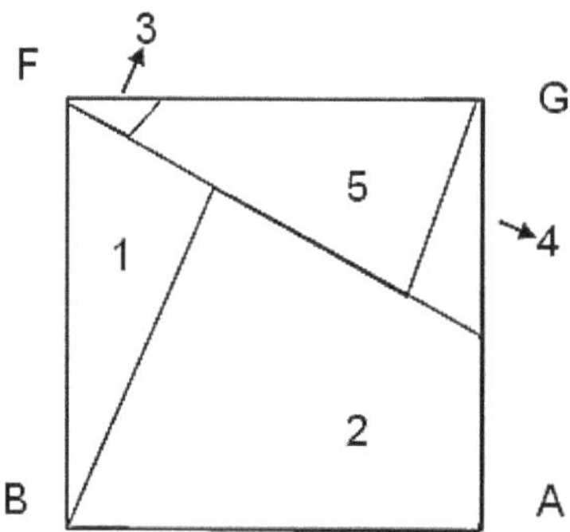

OBSERVATION

Cut pieces of squares ACIH and BCDH and completely cover the square ABFG.

∴ Area of square ACIH = $\mathrm{AC}^2 = 9\ \mathrm{cm}^2$, Area of square BCDE= $\mathrm{BC}^2 = 16\ \mathrm{cm}^2$, Area of square ABFG = $\mathrm{AB}^2 = 25\ \mathrm{cm}^2$

$\therefore AB^2 = BC^2 + AC^2 = 25 = 9 + 16$

RESULT

Pythagoras theorem is verified.

LEARNING OUTCOME

Students will learn practically that in a right-angled triangle, the square of the hypotenuse is equal to the sum of the squares of the other two sides.

ACTIVITY TIME

1. The area of an equilateral triangle described on the hypotenuse of a right-angled triangle is equal to the sum of the areas of equilateral triangles described on the other two sides.

   In ΔACD, $AC = DC = DA = 5cm$,

   $ar(\Delta ACD) = \frac{\sqrt{3}}{4}(5)^2$

   In ΔABE, $AB = BE = EA = 3cm$

   $ar(\Delta ABE) = \frac{\sqrt{3}}{4}(3)^2$

   In ΔBCF, $BC = CF = FB = 4cm$,

   $ar\ (BCF) = \frac{\sqrt{3}}{4}(4)^2$

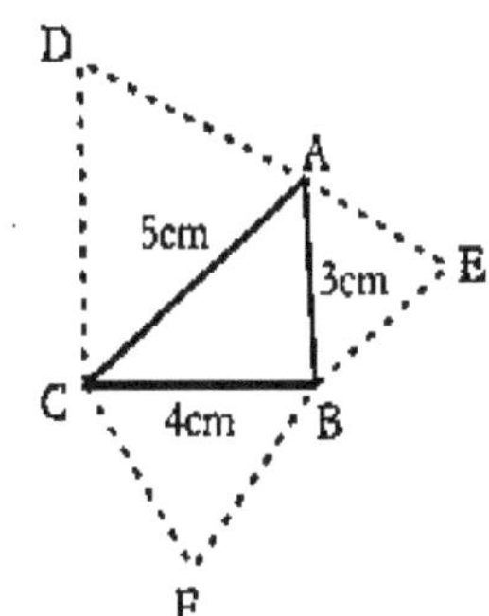

   Now, $ar(\Delta ABE) + ar(\Delta BCF) = \frac{\sqrt{3}}{4}(3)^2 + \frac{\sqrt{3}}{4}(4)^2$

   $= \frac{\sqrt{3}}{4}[9 + 16]$

   $= \frac{\sqrt{3}}{4}[25]$

   $= \frac{\sqrt{3}}{4}(5)^2$

   $\therefore ar(\Delta ABE) + ar(\Delta BCF) = ar(\Delta ACD)$ verified.

2. The area of a semi-circle described on the hypotenuse of a right-angled triangle is equal to the sum of the areas of semicircles described on the other two sides of the right-angled triangle.

   (Try yourself)

VIVA-VOCE

Question 1. What is the name given to the longest side of a right-angled triangle?
Answer: Hypotenuse.

Question 2. Name three sides of a right-angled triangle.
Answer: Base, perpendicular, the hypotenuse

Question 3. Is the Pythagoras theorem applicable for an equilateral triangle?
Answer: No.

Question 4. What is the name of the triplet forming the sides of a right-angled triangle?
Answer: Pythagorean triplet.

Question 5. Write the converse of the Pythagoras theorem.
Answer: In a triangle, if a square of the longest side is equal to the sum of the squares of the other two sides, then the angle opposite to the longest side is a right angle.

Question 6. Which of the following are Pythagorean triplets?
(a) $(3, 4, 6)$
(b) $(5, 12, 13)$
(c) $(6, 8, 10)$
Answer: (b), (c)

Question 7. If AC is the hypotenuse of a right-angled triangle ABC, then which angle will be a right angle?
Answer: Angle B.

Question 8. Can we prove the Pythagoras theorem for an acute-angled triangle or obtuse-angled triangle?
Answer: No.

Question 9. Who was the founder of the Pythagoras theorem?
Answer: Famous Greek philosopher, Pythagoras.

Question 10. ABC is an Isosceles triangle with $AC = BC$. If $AB^2 = 2AC^2$ then ABC is a right triangleand $\angle B = 90°$.

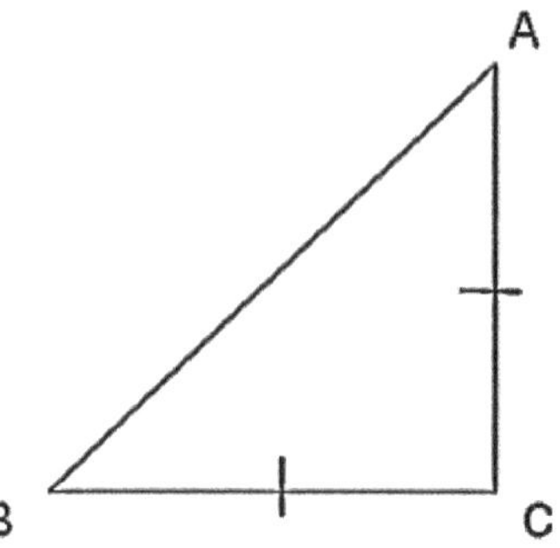

Answer: No, $\angle C = 90°$.

Question 11. If the side of the rhombus is 13 cm and one of its diagonals is 24 cm, then what will be the length of the other diagonal?
Answer: 10 cm

MULTIPLE CHOICE QUESTION

Question 1.
Find all angles of an isosceles right-angled triangle.
(a) $30°, 60°, 90°$
(b) $20°, 70°, 90°$
(c) $45°, 45°, 90°$
(d) none of these

Question 2.
In right ΔABC, $AB = 3cm$, $BC = 4$ cm and $\angle B = 90°$, then AC is
(a) 7 cm
(b) 5 cm
(c) 2 cm
(d) 3 cm

Question 3.
The hypotenuse of a right triangle is 17 cm long. If one of the remaining two sides is of length 8 cm. Then the length of another side
(a) 8 cm
(b) 12 cm
(c) 15 cm
(d) 24 cm

Question 4.
The sides of certain triangles are given below. Determine which of them are right triangles
(a) 7 cm, 24 cm, 25 cm
(b) 5 cm, 8 cm, 11 cm
(c) 5 cm, 20 cm, 25 cm
(d) none of these

Question 5.
ABC is an isosceles triangle, right angled at C. Tick the correct relation
(a) $2AB = AC^2$
(b) $BC = 2AB^2$
(c) $2AB^2 = AC^2 + BC^2$
(d) none of these

Question 6.
In ΔABC, $AB = 6\sqrt{3}$ cm, $AC = 12$ cm, and $BC = 6$ cm. The angle B is
(a) $120°$
(b) $60°$
(c) $90°$
(d) $45°$

Question 7.

The two legs of a right triangle are equal, and the square of the hypotenuse is 50, then the length of each leg is

(a) 13

(b) 5

(c) 10

(d) none of these

Question 8.

In ΔABC, $BD \perp AC$ and $\angle B = 90°$, then

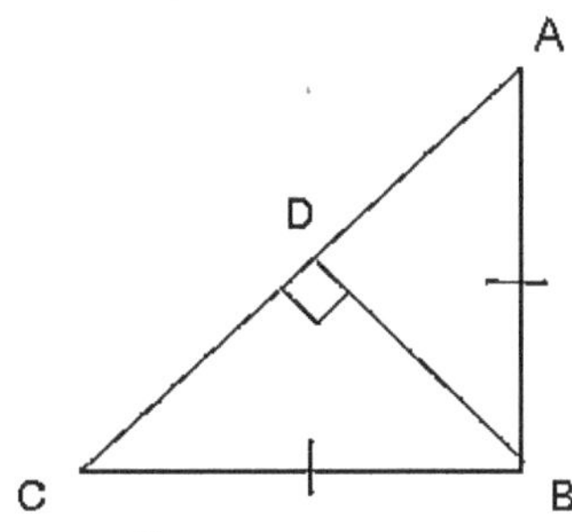

(a) $BD^2 = AD \times CD$

(b) $CD^2 = AD \times BD$

(c) $AD^2 = BD \times CD$

(d) none of these

Question 9.

ΔPQR is an equilateral triangle with each side of length $2p$. If $PS \perp QR$, then PS is equal to

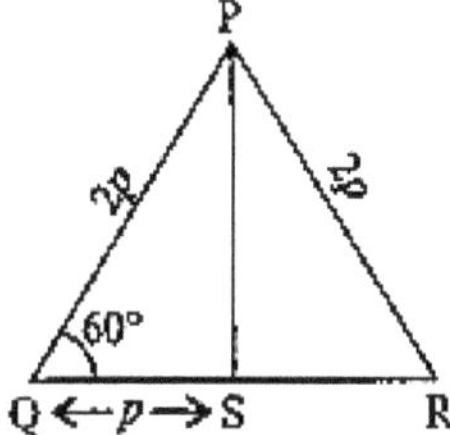

(a) $\frac{\sqrt{3}}{2}p$

(b) p

(c) $\sqrt{3}\ p$

(d) $2p$

Question 10.

A man goes 15m due west and then 8 m due north. How far is he from the starting point?

(a) 17m

(b) 9 m

(c) 12m

(d) 13 m

Answer Key

1.(c)	2.(b)	3.(b)	4.(a)	5.(d)	6.(c)	7.(b)	8.(a)	9.(c)	10.(a)

RATION OF AREAS OF TWO SIMILAR TRIANGLE

OBJECTIVE

To verify The ratio of the areas of two similar triangles is equal to the ratio of the square of their corresponding sides by performing an activity.

MATERIAL REQUIRED

Chart paper, construction box, coloured pens, a pair of scissors, fevicol.

THEORY

1. Concept of parallel lines.
2. Division of a line in a given ratio.

PROCEDURE

1. Take a chart paper and cut a ΔABC with $AB = 6cm$, $BC = 6cm$, $CA = 6cm$.
2. Mark 5 points P_1, P_2, ..., P_5 at a distance of 1cm each on side AB and Q_1,Q_2...., Q_5 at a distance of $1cm$ each on side AC as shown in fig (i).

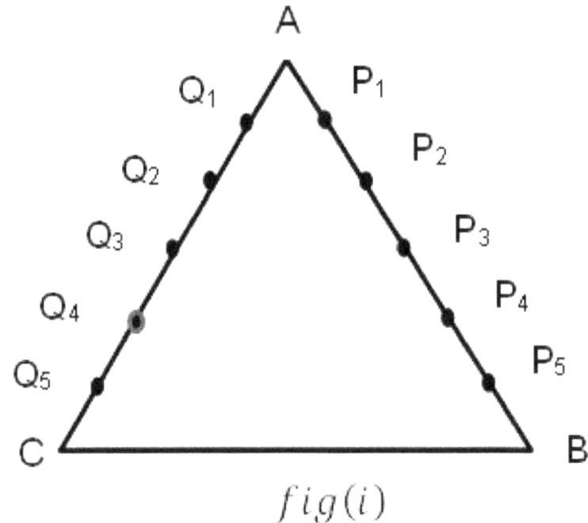

$fig(i)$

3. Join P_1Q_1, P_2Q_2,....................P_5Q_5as shown in fig (ii).

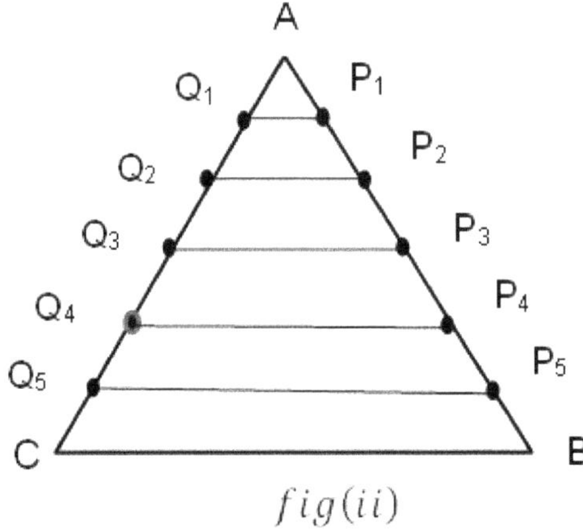

$fig(ii)$

4. Draw lines parallel to AC from P_1, P_2,.... P_5 and draw lines parallel to ABfrom the points Q_1, Q_2..., Q_5 as shown in fig (iii).

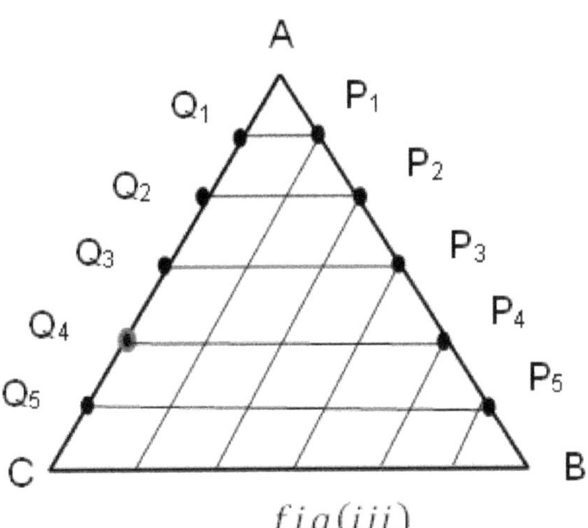

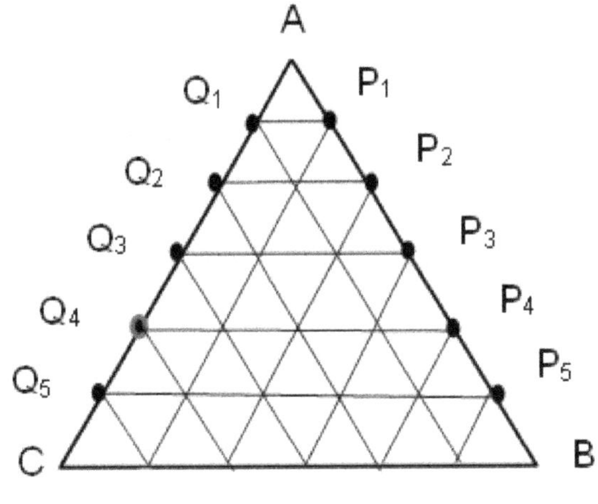

fig(iii)

5. Thus ΔABC is divided into 36 smaller triangles, and all are similar to each other and of equal area.
6. Construct a ΔPQR with $PQ = \frac{1}{2}$ of AB, $PR = \frac{1}{2}$ of AC and $QR = \frac{1}{2}$ of BC i.e.,3cm each on another chart paper.
7. Mark D_1, D_2 and E_1, E_2 on sides PQ and PR respectively.
8. Repeat steps 3 and 4.
9. Thus ΔPQR is divided into 9 smaller similar triangles equal in area.

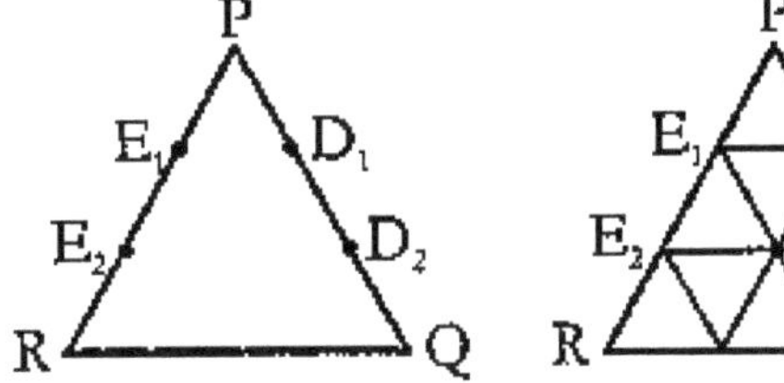

OBSERVATION

1. area of ΔABC = area of 36 smaller Δ's
2. area of ΔPQR = area of 9 smaller Δ's
3. $\frac{PQ}{AB} = \frac{3}{6} = \frac{1}{2} = \frac{PR}{AC}$
4. $\frac{\text{Area of } \Delta PQR}{\text{Area of } \Delta ABC} = \frac{PQ^2}{AB^2}$

   9 smaller Δ' s /36 smaller Δ' s $= \frac{1}{4} = (1/2)^2$

   (because $\triangle ABC \sim \triangle PQR$)

RESULT

Thus, it is verified that the ratio of the areas of two similar triangles is equal to the ratio of the square of their corresponding sides.

LEARNING OUTCOME

The concept of the area theorem is clear to the students through this activity.

ACTIVITY TIME

Take isosceles similar triangles and scalene similar triangles and try to verify this activity. Here isosceles triangles, $\Delta ABC \sim \Delta PQR$. Scalene triangle $\Delta DEF \sim \Delta KLM$

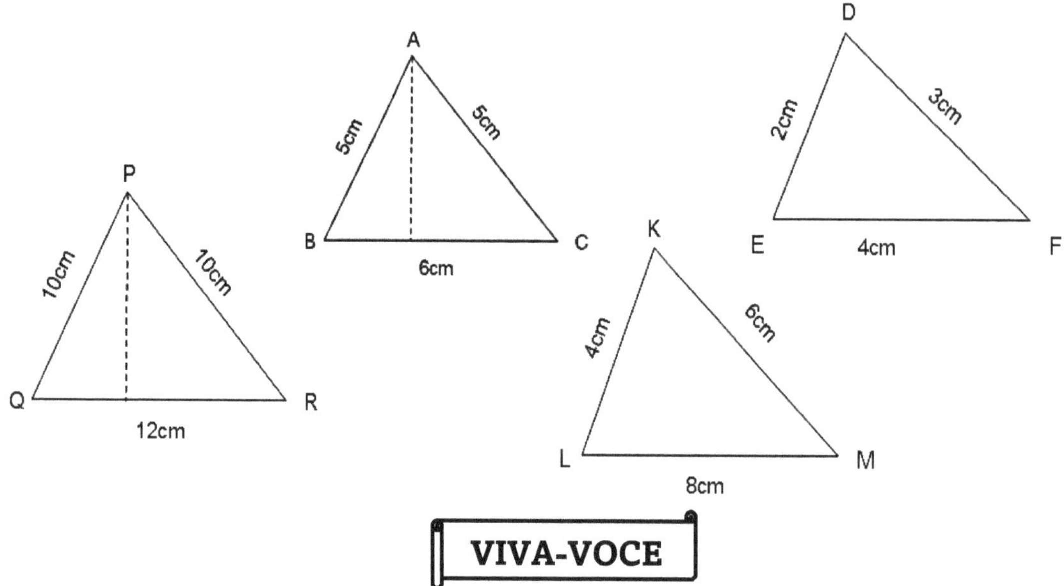

VIVA-VOCE

Question 1. What are the criteria for two triangles to be similar?
Answer: Two triangles are said to be similar if
- their corresponding angles are equal.
- their corresponding sides are in proportion

Question 2. ΔABC ~ ΔDEF and their areas are respectively 64 cm^2 and 121 cm^2. If EF = 15.4 cm,then find BC.
Answer: 11.2 cm

Question 3. Is it true, if the areas of two similar triangles are equal, then they are congruent?
Answer: Yes

Question 5. Are a square and a rhombus of side 3 cm similar?
Answer: No

Question 4. What is the ratio of the area of an equilateral triangle described on one side of a square to the area of an equilateral triangle described on one of its diagonals?
Answer: 1:2

Question 6. Is a rhombus of side 3 cm congruent to another rhombus of side 4 cm?
Answer: No

Question 7. Is the ratio of the areas of two similar triangles equal to the square of the ratio oftheir corresponding medians?
Answer: Yes

Question 10. Area of an equilateral triangle with side length a is equal to:
Answer: $\sqrt{3/4}\, a^2$

MULTIPLE CHOICE QUESTION

Question 1.
ABC and BDE are two equilateral triangles, such that D is the mid-point of BC. The the ratio of the areas of $\Delta\mathrm{ABC}$ and $\Delta\mathrm{BDE}$ is
(a) 4:1
(b) 1:4
(c) 1:2
(d) 2:1

Question 2.
If in two similar triangles PQR and LMN, if $\mathrm{QR} = 15\ \mathrm{cm}$ and $\mathrm{MN} = 10\ \mathrm{cm}$, then the ratio of the areas of triangles is
(a) $3:2$
(b) $9:4$
(c) $5:4$
(d) $7:4$

Question 3.
The sides of two similar triangles are in the ratio $4:9$. Areas of these triangles are in the ratio
(a) $2:3$
(b) $4:9$
(c) $81:16$
(d) $16:81$

Question 4.
Two isosceles triangles have equal vertical angles, and their areas are in the ratio $16:25$. Then the ratio of their corresponding heights is
(a) $16:25$
(b) $256:625$
(c) $4:5$
(d) none of these

Question 5.
$\Delta ABC \sim \Delta DEF$. If $AC = 19$ cm and $DF = 8$ cm, then the ratio of the areas of the two triangles are
(a) $361:64$
(b) $19:8$
(c) $19:4$
(d) none of these

Question 6.
ΔDEF ~ ΔABC; If DE: AB = 2: 3 and area ΔDEF is equal to 44 square units, then area(ΔABC) is
(a) 120 sq. units
(b) 99 sq. units
(c) 66 sq. units
(d) none of these

Question 7.
Diagonals of a trapezium ABCD with AB || DC intersect each other at the point O. IfAB = 2CD, find the ratio of the areas of triangles AOB and COD.
(a) $4:1$
(b) $1:4$
(c) $4:4$
(d) $2:4$

Question 8.
In the given figure, PB and QA are perpendicular to segment AB. If PO = 5 cm, QO = 7 cm and area $(\Delta POB) = 150\ cm^2$, then area of ΔQOA is

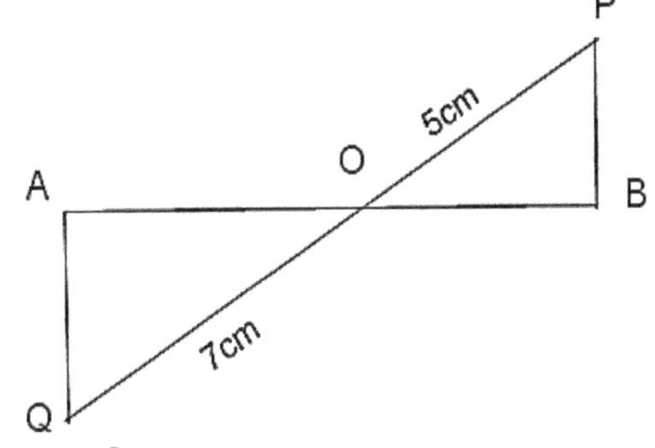

(a) $254\ cm^2$
(b) $294\ cm^2$
(c) $244\ cm^2$
(d) $49\ cm^2$

Question 9.
ABC and DBC are two triangles on the same base BC. If AD intersects BC at O, then the ratio of the area (ΔABC) to the area (ΔDBC) is
(a) $\frac{AO}{DO}$
(b) $\frac{AO}{DB}$
(c) $\frac{AC}{DO}$
(d) none of these

Question 10.
Area (ΔABC): Area $(\Delta DEF) = 25:36$. Then AB: DE is
(a) $625:1296$
(b) $25:36$
(c) $6:5$
(d) $5:6$

Answer Key

1.(c)	2.(b)	3.(d)	4.(c)	5.(a)	6.(b)	7.(a)	8.(b)	9.(a)	10.(d)

ACTIVITY 8

CENTROID OF A TRIANGLE

OBJECTIVE
To find the centroid of a triangle using paper cutting and folding activity.

MATERIAL REQUIRED
Coloured papers, a pair of scissors, pencil, geometry box, fevistick.

THEORY
1. Concept of finding the mid-point of a line segment by paper folding.
2. Definition of medians.
3. Meaning of Centroid.

PROCEDURE
1. Cut an acute-angled triangle ABC from a coloured sheet of paper.

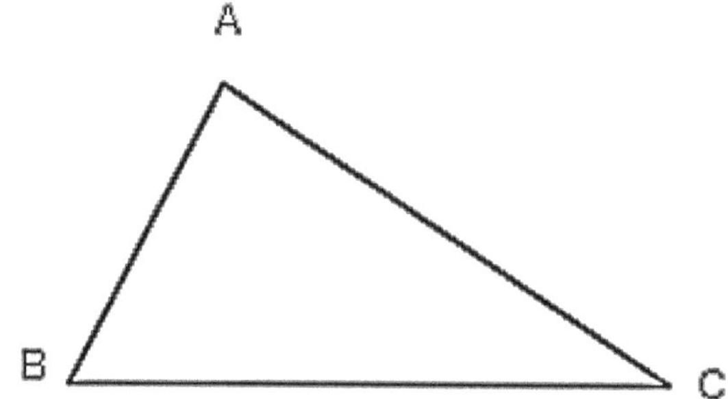

2. Find the mid-points of sides AB, BC and AC by paper folding.

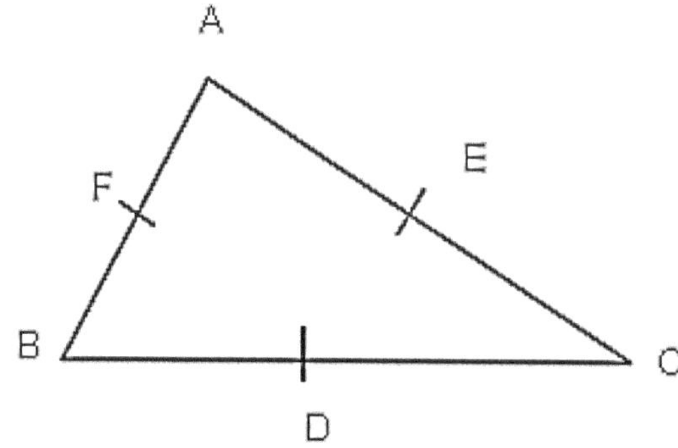

3. Fold the triangle along with AD, press it and unfold it, along with BE, press it and unfold it, similarly fold the triangle along with CF, fold it press it and unfold it.
4. We get three creases AD, BE and CE These three creases are called medians and they meet or intersect or pass through one point say G.

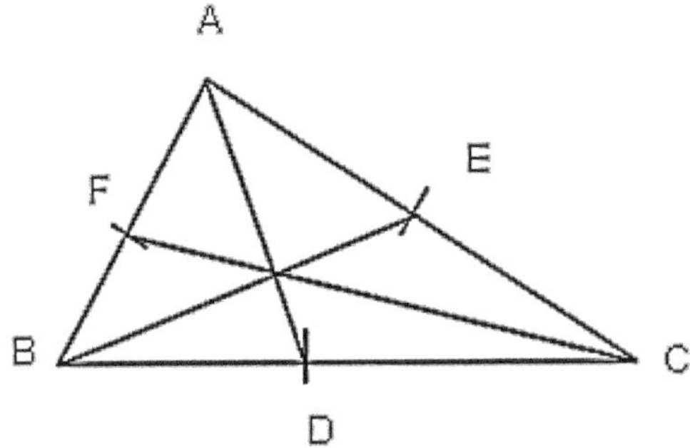

5. This point G is known as the centroid of an ΔABC.

OBSERVATION

1. We get three medians of ΔABC as AD, BE and CF.
2. The point of concurrence is known as the centroid of an ΔABC.

RESULT

All three medians in a triangle intersect at a point called the centroid of the triangle.

LEARNING OUTCOME

Medians of an acute-angled triangle concurred at a point known as centroid, which always lies inside the triangle

ACTIVITY TIME

Verify that the centroid of an obtuse-angled triangle and a right-angled triangle always lie inside the triangle.

VIVA-VOCE

Question 1. Define centroid.
Answer: It is the point of concurrence of all three medians of a triangle.

Question 2. Does the centroid lie outside the triangle?
Answer: No. It always lies inside the triangle.

Question 3. In what ratio, the centroid divides the median from vertex to mid-point of the opposite side?
Answer: 2: 1

Question 4. Define median.
Answer: A line segment joining a vertex to the mid-point of its opposite side is known as a median.

Question 5. Is it correct to say that all three medians in a triangle are the same in length?
Answer: No

Question 6. In an equilateral triangle PQR, G is the centroid. What is the relationship between the areas of ΔGPQ, ΔGQR and ΔGPR?
Answer: $ar(\Delta GPQ) = ar(\Delta GQR) = ar(\Delta GPR)$

Question 7. Are three angle bisectors of a triangle meet at a point?
Answer: Yes (at in Centre)

Question 8. Tell the number of medians in a triangle.
Answer: 3

MULTIPLE CHOICE QUESTION

Question 1.
In a triangle, the centroid divides medians of the triangle in the ratio
(a) $1:2$
(b) $2:1$
(c) $2:3$
(d) none of these

Question 2. In a triangle ABC, if BD and AE are two medians that intersect at M. If BM = 6 cm,what is the value of BD?
(a) 10 cm
(b) 2 cm
(c) 9 cm
(d) none of these

Question 3.
In a triangle EFG, if EP and FQ are two medians intersecting at M such that $\text{MP} = 8 \text{ cm}$, then the value of EM will be '
(a) 16 cm
(b) 4 cm
(c) 12 cm
(d) none of these

Question 4.
If PM and QR are two medians intersecting inside the ΔPQS at the point G, such that $\text{QG} = 5 \text{ cm}$, then GR will be
(a) 2.5 cm
(b) 10 cm
(c) 4.5 cm
(d) none of these

Question 5.
In a right triangle PQS right-angled at Q if PQ = 4 cm, QS = 6 cm, and PR and QT are two medians intersecting at G, what will be the value of PG?
(a) $\frac{15}{2} \text{cm}$
(b) $\frac{10}{3} \text{cm}$
(c) $\frac{15}{3} \text{cm}$
(d) none of these

Question 6.
In an isosceles right-angled triangle ABC, if the length of each of the two equal sides is 6 cm, and the two medians AP and CQ intersect at M, the value of MQ will be
(a) $\sqrt{5} \text{ cm}$
(b) $2\sqrt{5} \text{ cm}$
(c) $5\sqrt{5} \text{ cm}$
(d) none of these

Question 7.
In an equilateral triangle ABC of side 6 cm, if two medians BP and CQ intersect eachother inside the triangle at G, then the length of the median will be
(a) $3\sqrt{3}\text{cm}$
(b) different in length
(c) $5\sqrt{3} \text{ cm}$
(d) none of these

Question 8.
In an isosceles triangle ABC, BD and CE are medians intersecting at M. If $\text{CE} = 6\text{cm}$, what will be the value of other median BD?
(a) 3 cm
(b) 6 cm
(c) 4 cm
(d) none of these

Question 9.
What will be the position of the centroid in an isosceles right-angled triangle?
(a) inside
(b) outside
(c) on the triangle
(d) none of these

Question 10.
In an equilateral triangle, the lengths of three medians will be
(a) different
(b) can't say
(c) same
(d) none of these

Answer Key

1.(b)	2.(c)	3.(a)	4.(a)	5.(b)	6.(a)	7.(a)	8.(b)	9.(a)	10.(c)

ACTIVITY 9

MAKING OF A CLINOMETER

OBJECTIVE

To make a mathematical instrument 'clinometer' to measure the height of a distant object.

MATERIAL REQUIRED

Small pipe or drinking straw, a wooden board, wooden strip, thread, weight, screw,geometry box, etc.

THEORY

1. Concept of the angle of elevation and depression.
2. Properties of a right-angled triangle.

PROCEDURE

1. Prepare a semi-circular protractor with the help of a geometry box. Mark degrees in sexagesimal scale with $0°$ at the lowest and $10°$ to $90°$ proceeding both clockwise and anti-clockwise.
2. Fix a hollow pipe along the diameter of its fig.
3. Punch a hole at the Centre of a semicircle.
4. Suspend a weight (w) from a small nail fixed to the Centre.
5. Ensure that the weight at the end of the string hangs below the protractor.

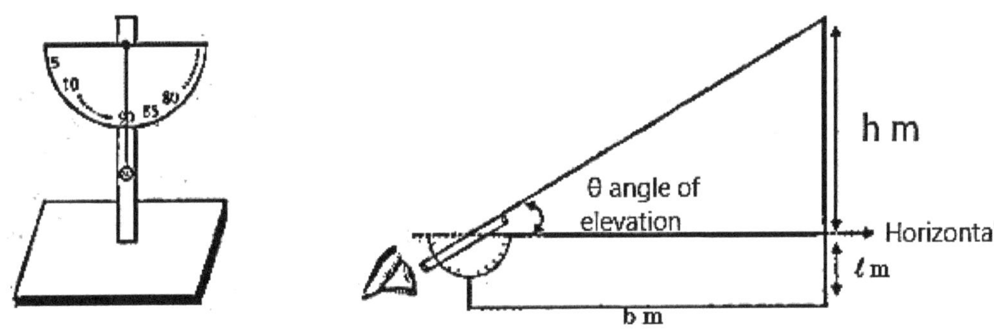

DETERMINING THE HEIGHT OF AN OBJECT:

1. Measure the distance of the object from you. Let it is d.
2. Look through the hollow pipe straw at the top of the object by rotating it gradually.Make sure that you can see the top of the object.
3. Hold the clinometer steady and record the angle that the string makes on the scale of the clinometer. This angle is the required angle of elevation, let be θ. Using trigonometric ratio:

$$\tan\,\theta = \frac{\text{height}}{\text{distance}} = \frac{h}{d}$$
$$\text{h} = \text{d} \cdot \tan\,\theta$$

OBSERVATION

1. angle of elevation $0°$.

2. distance between object and clinometer d.
3. height of clinometer ($l\ m$)

Therefore, height of object $= l + h = l + d \tan \theta$

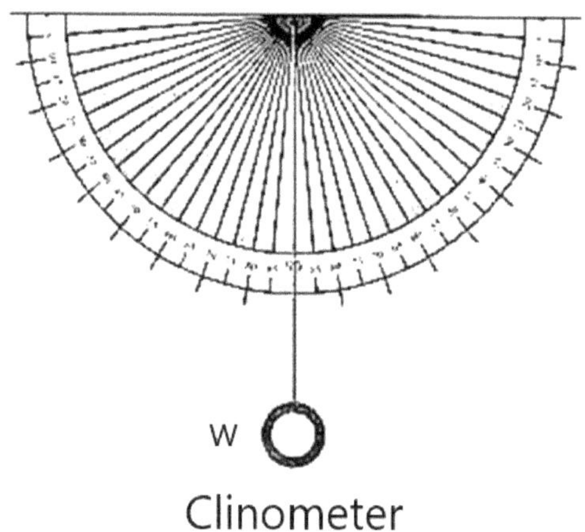

Clinometer

RESULT

The angle of elevation can be found easily.

LEARNING OUTCOME

Students learn how to determine the angle of elevation of an object by clinometer and use it to determine the height of an object at a known distance.

ACTIVITY TIME

1. If the height of the clinometer is 3 m, the distance between object and clinometer is 27 m and the angle of elevation is 45°. What is the height of anobject?
2. A kite is flying at a height of $40\sqrt{3}$ meter from the ground level, attached to a string inclined at 60° to the horizontal. What is the length of the string?

VIVA-VOCE

Question 1. What is the value of $\frac{\sin 18^0}{\cos 72^0}$?
Answer: 1

Question 2. How many trigonometric ratios are there for an acute angle in a right-angled triangle?
Answer: 6.

Question 3. If the angle of elevation of an object is 30°, then tan 0 (where 0 is the angle of elevation)is?
Answer: $\tan \theta = \tan 30° = \frac{1}{\sqrt{3}}$

Question 4. If $\tan A = \cot B$ then is it right A + B = 90°?
Answer: Yes.

Question 5. What is trigonometry?
Answer: It is an important branch of mathematics. In this branch, we deal with the relation and measurement of the sides and the angles of a triangle.

Question 6. How many trigonometric ratios are there for an acute angle in a right-angled triangle?
Answer: 6.

MULTIPLE CHOICE QUESTION

Question 1.

If $3 \cot A = 4$, then $\frac{1-\tan^2 A}{1+\tan^2 A}$ is equal to

(a) $\cos^2 A - \sin^2 A$

(b) $\sin^2 A - \cos^2 A$

(c) $\sin^2 A + \cos^2 A$

(d) none of these

Question 2.

In ΔABC, right-angled at B, if tan A $=\frac{1}{\sqrt{3}}$, then the value of sin A cos C + cos A sin C is

(a) 0

(b) 1

(c) 2

(d) none of these

Question 3.

In ΔABC right angled at C if ∠ A = ∠B, then which is correct?

(a) cos A = cos B

(b) cos A = cos C

(c) cos B = cos C

(d) none of these

Question 4.

Choose the correct option for, $\frac{2\tan 30^\circ}{1+\tan^2 30} =$

(a) $\sin 60^\circ$

(b) $\cos 60^\circ$

(c) $\tan 60^\circ$

(d) $\sin 30^\circ$

Question 5.

If sin (A + B) = 1, cos (A − B) = 1, 0° < A + B ≤90°, A ≥ B, then A and B are respectively

(a) 45° and 45°

(b) 45° and 15°

(c) 30° and 30°

(d) 30° and 15°

Question 6.

Choose the correct option for $9\sec^2 - 9\tan^2$

(a) 1

(b) 9

(c) 8

(d) 0

Question 7.

Choose the correct option for (sec A) (1 − sin A) (sec A + tan A).

(a) 1

(b) 2

(c) 0

(d) −1

Question 8.

A player sitting on the top of a tower of height 20 m observes the angle of depression of a ball tied on the ground as 60°. What is the distance between the footof the tower and the ball?

(a) 11.45 m

(b) 11.55 m

(c) 11.59 m

(d) none of these

Question 9.

A plane is observed to be approaching the airport. It is at a distance of 12 km from the point of observation and makes an angle of elevation of 30° at that point. What isits height above the ground?

(a) 5 km

(b) 4 km

(c) 6 km

(d) 7 km

Question 10.

If tan (60°−α) = 1, then α is

(a) 45°

(b) 15°

(c) 60°

(d) 30°

Question 11.

The value of $3\cos^2 30^\circ + \tan^2 60^\circ$ is

(a) $\frac{21}{4}$

(b) 5

(c) 1

(d) $6\frac{21}{4}$

Answer Key

1.(a)	2.(b)	3.(a)	4.(a)	5.(a)	6.(b)	7.(a)	8.(b)	9.(c)	10.(b)
11.(a)									

TANGENTS DRAWN FROM AN EXTERNAL POINT

OBJECTIVE

To verify experimentally that lengths of tangents drawn from an external point to a circle are equal.

TANGENT

A line touching the circle at a point is called a tangent to the circle.

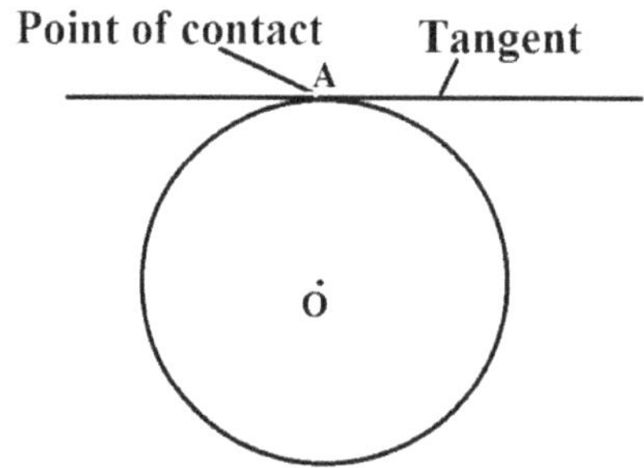

MATERIAL REQUIRED

Glazed papers, white chart paper, sketch pens, a pair of scissors, geometry box, fevicol.

THEORY

1. Tangent to a circle.
2. Length of a tangent.

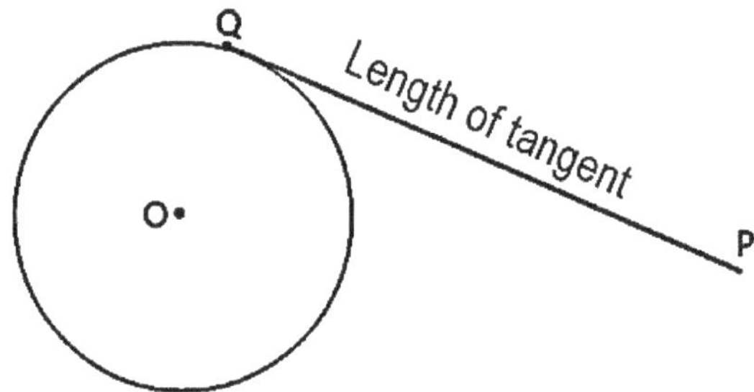

PROCEDURE

1. Cut a circle of any radius from a glazed paper and paste it on a whitechart paper.

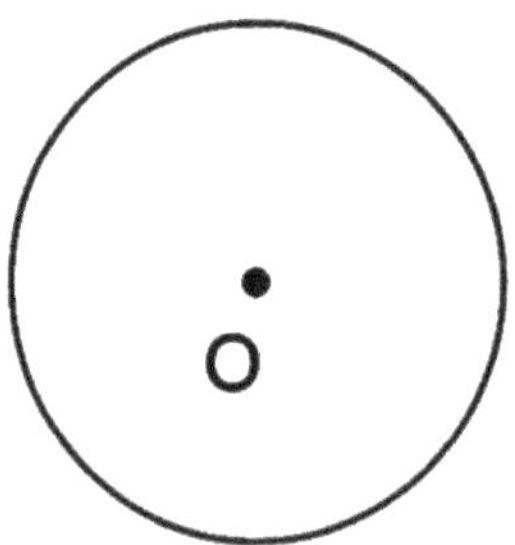

2. Take any point P on the circle.

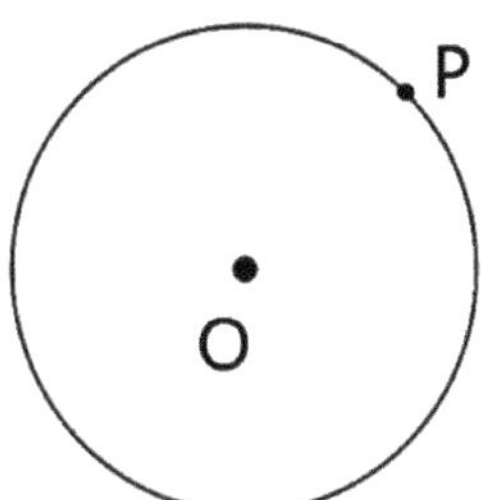

3. From P, fold the paper in such a way that it just touches the circle at P.Press it and unfold to get a tangent PA.

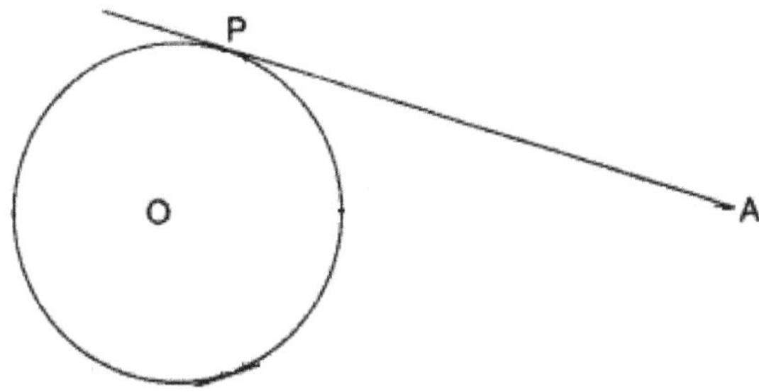

4. From A, fold the paper to get tangent AQ.

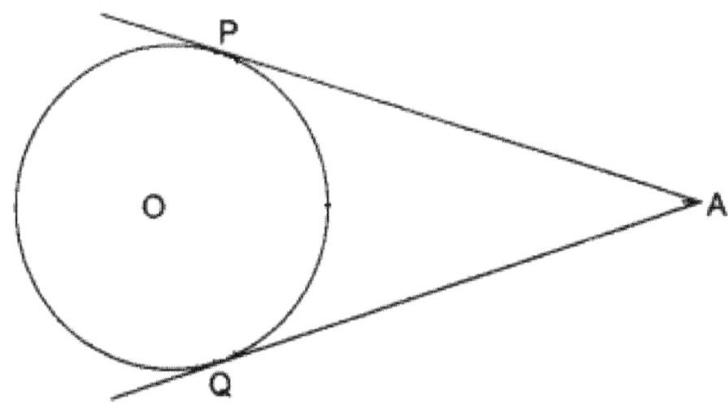

5. Fold the circle along with OA.
6. Join OP, OA, OQ.

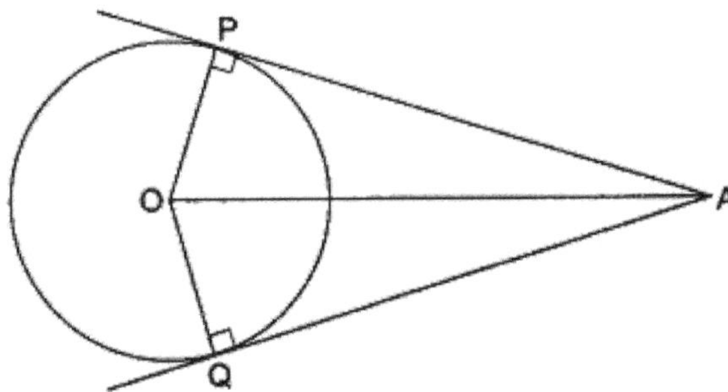

OBSERVATION

Students observe that point P coincide with Q

$\therefore$ AP = AQ

RESULT

Thus, it is verified that lengths of tangents drawn from an external point to a circle are equal.

LEARNING OUTCOME

Students will learn how to measure tangents from an external point to a circle byusing paper folding.

ACTIVITY TIME

1. Draw two tangents from a point P to a circle of radius 3 cm. If its distance from the Centre is 10 cm, measure the lengths of the tangents.Are they equal?
2. In the adjoining figure, prove that AD+BC = AB+CD

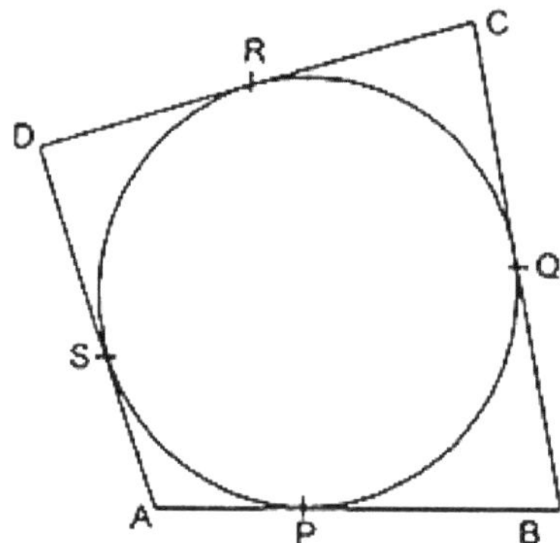

3. In the adjoining figure, find PQ and PR.

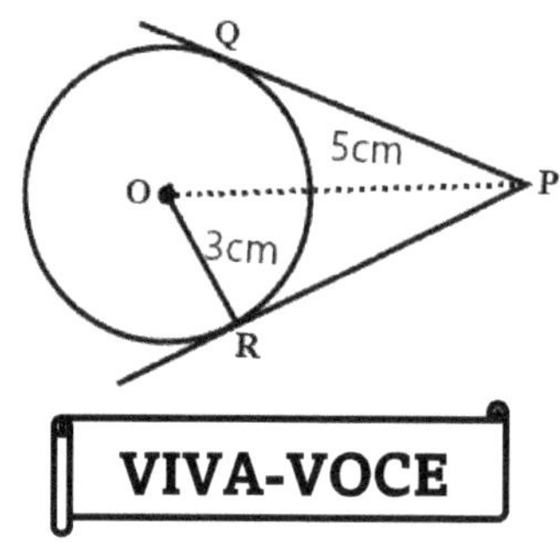

VIVA-VOCE

Question 1. Define tangent to a circle.
Answer: A-line touching the circle at one point is called a tangent to that circle.

Question 2. Is it possible that a line can touch the circle at more than one point?
Answer: No.

Question 3. How many tangents can be drawn to a circle from a common point outside the circle?
Answer: Two.

Question 4. Is it possible to draw a tangent from a point inside the circle?
Answer: No.

Question 5. Is it possible to draw two tangents of different lengths from a common external point?
Answer: No.

Question 6. Is a tangent at any point of a circle perpendicular to the radius through the point ofcontact?
Answer: Yes.

Question 7. In the fig., is $\sqrt{x} = \sqrt{y}$?

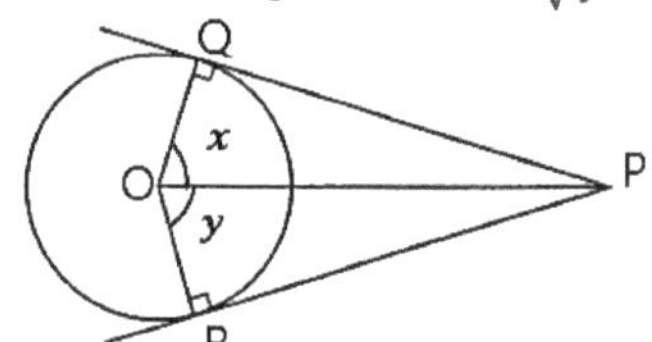

Answer: Yes.

Question 8. In the fig. is $\Delta POQ \cong \Delta POR$?

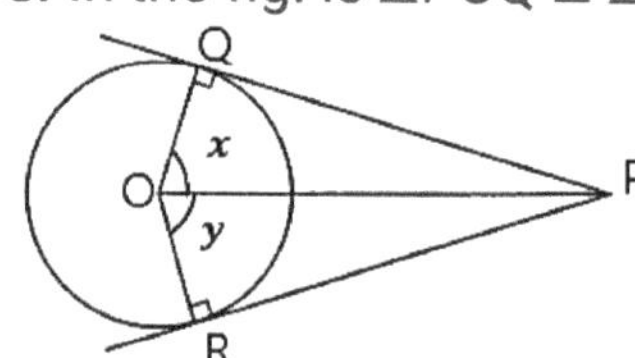

Answer: Yes.

MULTIPLE CHOICE QUESTION

Question 1.
The distance between two parallel tangents drawn to a circle is equal to the
(a) diameter of circle
(b) radius of circle
(c) twice of diameter
(d) none of these

Question 2.
At the point of contact, the angle between radius and tangent to a circle is
(a) $180°$
(b) $90°$
(c) acute angle
(d) none of these

Question 3.
A tangent PQ at a point P of a circle of radius 5 cm meets a line through the Centre Oat a point Q so that OQ= 12 cm. Length of PQ is
(a) 12 cm
(b) 13 cm
(c) 8.5 cm
(d) $\sqrt{119}$ cm

Question 4.
From a point Q, the length of the tangent to a circle is 24 cm and the distance of Q from the Centre is 25 cm. The radius of the circle is
(a) 7 cm
(b) 12 cm
(c) 15 cm
(d) 24.5 cm

Question 5.
TP and TQ are two tangents to a circle with Centre O, so that ∠POQ = 110°, then ∠PTQ is equal to
(a) 60° (c) 80°
(b) 70° (d) 90°

Question 6.
If tangent PA and PB from a point P to a circle with Centre O are inclined to eachother at an angle of 80°, then ∠POA is equal to
(a) 50° (c) 70°
(b) 60° (d) 80°

Question7.
In the figure, If PQ = PR, then which is correct

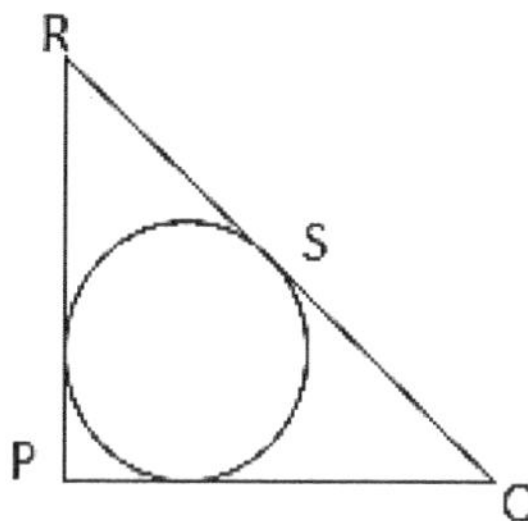

(a) $QS = SR$
(b) $QS = 2RS$
(c) $QS \neq RS$
(d) none of these

Question 8.
PQ and PR are tangents from point P to the circle with Centre O. N is a point on thecircle, then choose the correct relation.

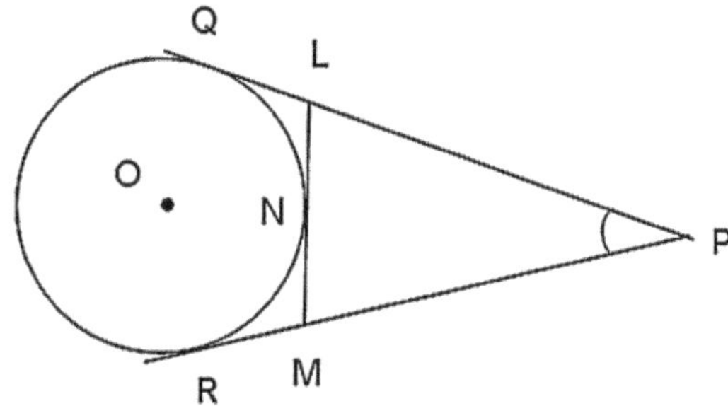

(a) $PL + MN = PM - LN$
(b) $PL + MN = PM + LN$
(c) $PL + PM = LN + MN$
(d) $PL + LN = PM + MN$

Question 9.
AB and AC are two tangents drawn to the circle with Centre O. If ∠BAC = 85° then ∠BOC is
(a) 95° (c) 90°
(b) 85° (d) 80°

Question 10.
Two concentric circles are of radii 5 cm and 3 cm. The length of the chord of the larger circle which touches the smaller circle is
(a) 5 cm
(b) 4 cm
(c) 6 cm
(d) 8 cm

Answer Key

1.(a)	2.(b)	3.(d)	4.(a)	5.(b)	6.(a)	7.(a)	8.(d)	9.(a)	10.(d)

ACTIVITY 11

AREA OF CIRCLE BY COILING METHOD

OBJECTIVE

To obtain the formula for area of a circle i.e., πr^2 by coiling method.

MATERIAL REQUIRED

Thick string or coloured threads, cutter, a pair of scissors, fevicol, geometry box.

THEORY

1. **Definition of the circle:** A circle is the locus of a point in a plane that moves in such a way that its distance from a fixed point remains constant. Fixed point is known as the Centre and the fixed distance is known as the radius of the circle.

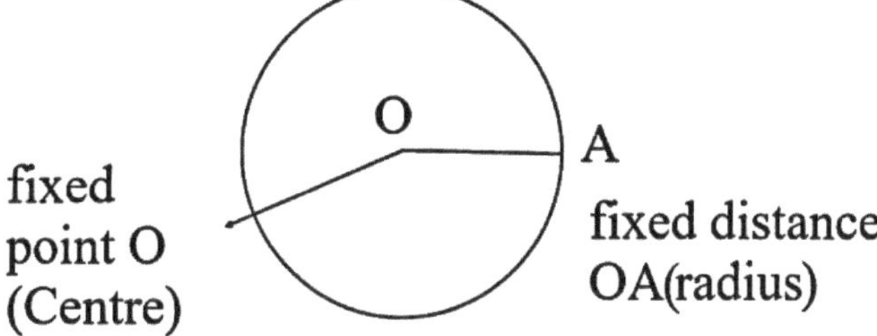

2. **Area of the circle:** It is the measure of the region of a plane enclosed by it.
3. **Circumference of the circle:** Total length of its boundary
   ($C = 2\pi r$, where r is the radius of the circle)

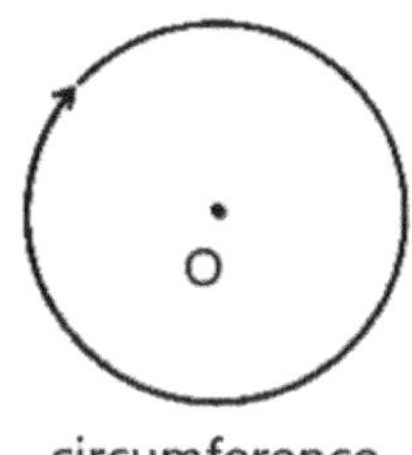

4. **Area of a triangle:** $\frac{1}{2} \times$ Base $\times$ height
5. **Concentric circles:** Circles having the same Centre.

PROCEDURE

1. Construct a circle of radius r, (take r = 3.5 cm) using a compass and draw concentric circles of smaller radius as shown in fig.

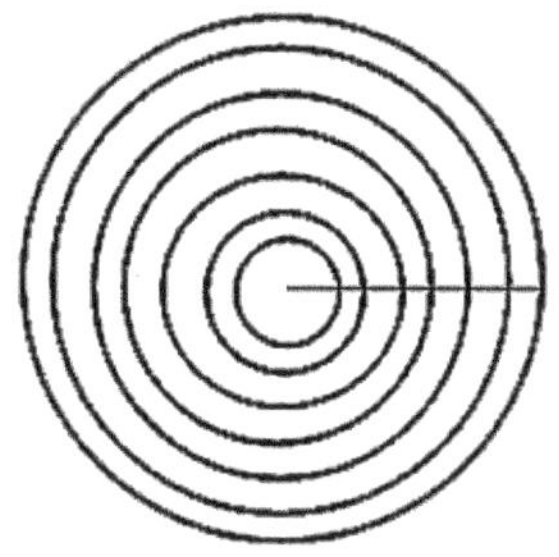

2. Fill the area of the drawn circle with concentric circles made of different coloured strings or thread, so that there is no gap between the threads as shown in fig.

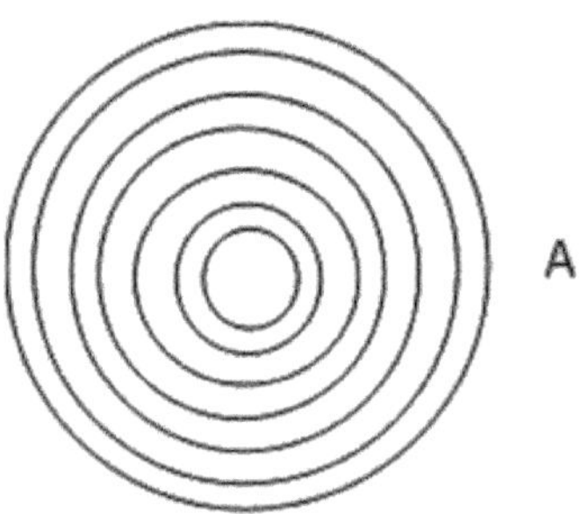

3. Last smallest circle be a point circle.
4. With the help of scissors, cut the coloured circular threads along the radius OA.
5. Open all the threads and arrange each thread as a straight line.
6. Place each thread one over another starting from the thread of the largest circle to the smallest circle in such a way that it forms a triangular shape as shown in fig.

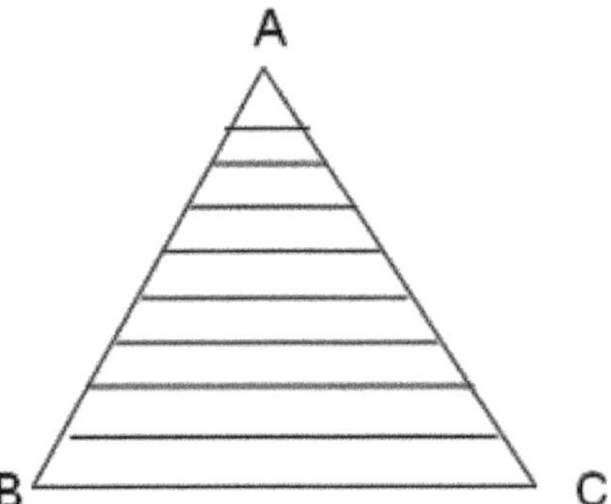

OBSERVATION

1. The triangular shape so formed out of the threads; the area of the circle is the same as the area of the triangular shape.
2. Base of the triangle is the circumference of the circle (The largest thread) i.e., Base of $\Delta = 2\pi r$
3. Vertical height of the triangular shape = radius of the circle.

$$\text{Area of } \Delta = \frac{1}{2} \times B \times H$$
$$= \frac{1}{2} \times 2\pi r \times r$$
$$= \pi r^2$$

$\therefore$ area of the circle of radius $r = \pi r^2$

RESULT

The figure formed in this activity is almost the shape of the triangle, therefore the area of this triangle so formed is equal to the area of the circle i.e., πr^2 sq. units.

LEARNING OUTCOME

Students observe that the area of the circle is πr^2 i.e., half the product of its circumference and radius.

ACTIVITY TIME

1. Using the above activity find the area of the circle taking radius as 4.2 cm.
2. Using the above activity find the area of the circle taking radius as 4.9 cm.

VIVA-VOCE

Question 1. What is the area of the rectangle?
Answer: Area of rectangle = length × breadth

Question 2. Mention the area of the circle in terms of diameter.
Answer: Area of circle = $\frac{\pi d^2}{4}$, where d is the diameter of the circle.

Question 3. What is the formula to find the area of a sector of a circle of radius r and its central? angle θ?
Answer: Area of a sector with central angle $\theta = \frac{\pi r^2 \theta}{360^0}$.

Question 4. How will you define a circle?
Answer: A circle is the locus of a point in a plane that moves in such a way that its distancefrom a fixed point remains constant. The fixed point is known as the Centre of the circle and the fixed distance is known as the radius of the circle.

MULTIPLE CHOICE QUESTION

Question 1.
Find the central angle of a circle of radius 21 cm if the length of the arc is 22 cm.
(a) 30°
(b) 60°
(c) 45°
(d) 100°

Question 2.
If the area of a minor segment of a circle is π cm^2 and radius is 7 cm, then what is the area of its major segment?
(a) 48π cm^2
(b) 49π cm^2
(c) 7πcm^2
(d) none of these

Question 3.
Find out the length of a circular arc subtending an angle of 60° at the Centre and radius 14 cm.
(a) 14 cm
(b) 44 cm
(c) $\frac{44}{3}$ cm
(d) none of these

Question 4.
If a thread of length a cm is converted into a circle, then find its area.
(a) $\frac{a}{4\pi}$
(b) $\frac{a^2}{4}$
(c) $\frac{a^2}{4\pi^2}$
(d) $\frac{a^2}{4\pi}$

Question 5.
Find the area of a ring shown in the figure if OA =10 cm and OB = 8 cm.

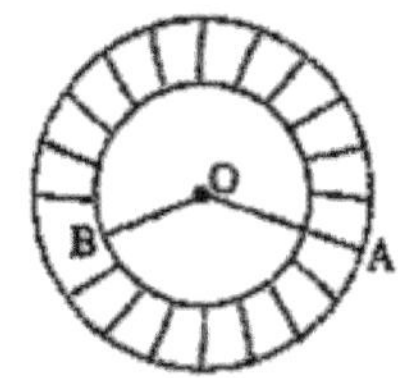

(a) 30πcm^2
(b) 36πcm^2
(c) 18πcm^2
(d) none of these

Answer Key

1.(b)	2.(a)	3.(c)	4.(d)	5.(b)

ACTIVITY 12 AREA OF CIRCLE BY PAPER CUTTING AND PASTING METHOD

OBJECTIVE

To obtain the formula for the area of the circle i.e., πr^2 by paper cutting and pasting method.

MATERIAL REQUIRED

White paper, coloured sketch pen, a pair of scissors, fevicol, geometry box.

THEORY

1. **Definition of the circle:** A circle is the locus of a point in a plane that moves in such a way that its distance from a fixed point remains constant. The fixed point is known as the Centre and the fixed distance is known as the radius of the circle.

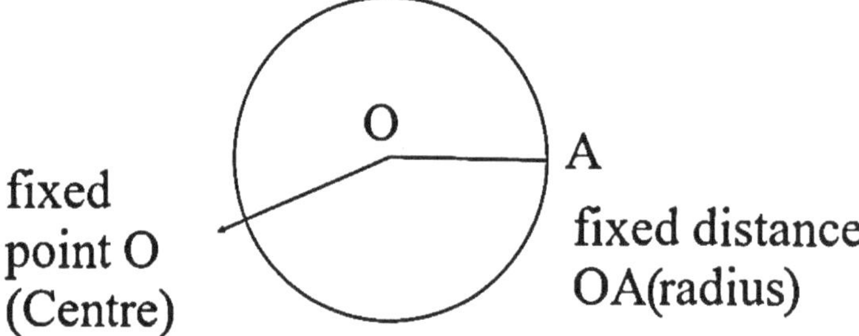

2. **Area of the circle:** It is the measure of the region of the plane enclosed by it.
3. **Circumference of the circle:** Total length of its boundary.
   ($C = 2\pi r$, where r is the radius of the circle)

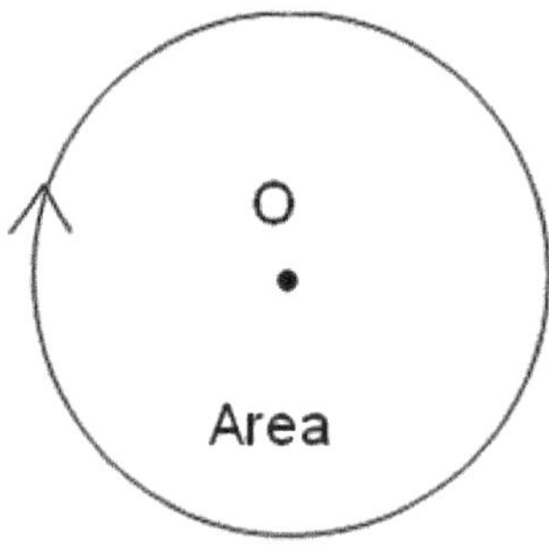

Circumference

4. **Area of rectangle:** length × breadth.
5. **Sectors of a circle.**

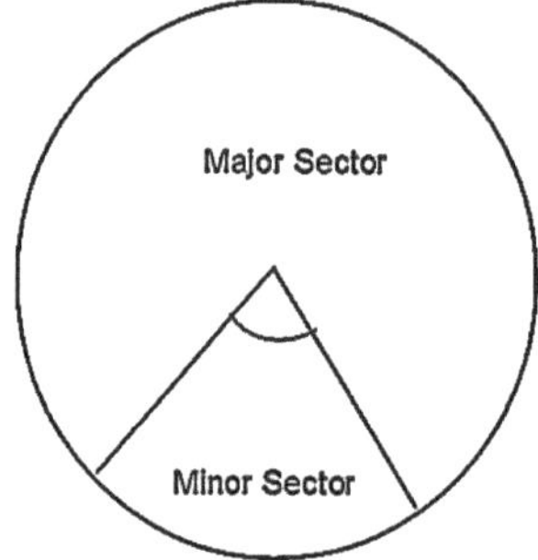

PROCEDURE

1. Draw a circle of any radius on a sheet of paper (Take $r = 6.5$ cm) using a compass.

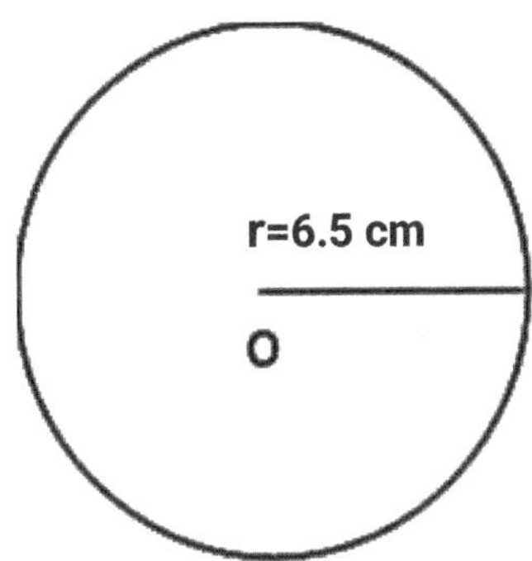

2. Fold it once along the diameter to obtain two semicircles as shown in fig.

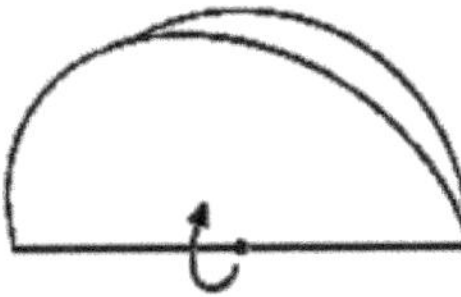
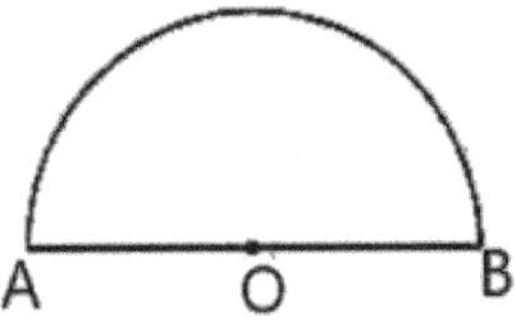

3. Again, fold the semicircle to get quarters of the circle.

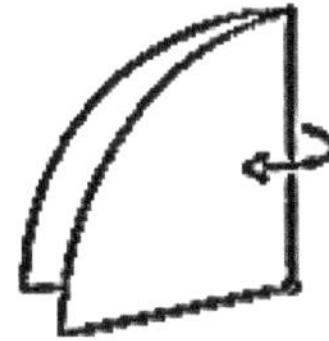
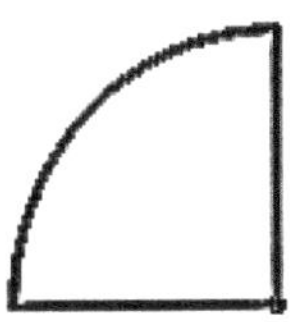

4. Repeat this process of folding up to four folds and then it looks like a small sector as shown in fig.

5. Press and unfold the circle. It is divided into 16 equal sectors.
6. Colour half of this circle i.e., 8 parts with one sector with colour say blue and remaining 8 sectors different colour say orange.

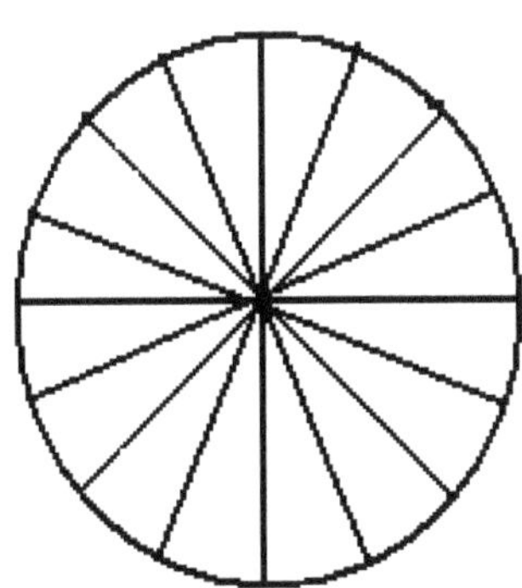

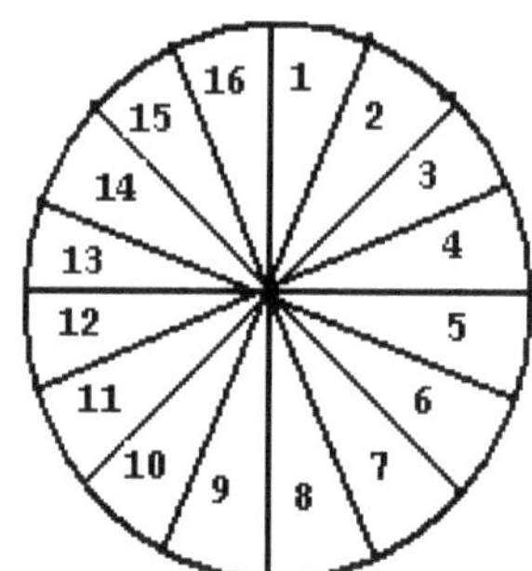

7. Cut these sixteen different sectors of the circle.
8. Cut one of the sectors of orange colour into two equal parts as shown in fig.

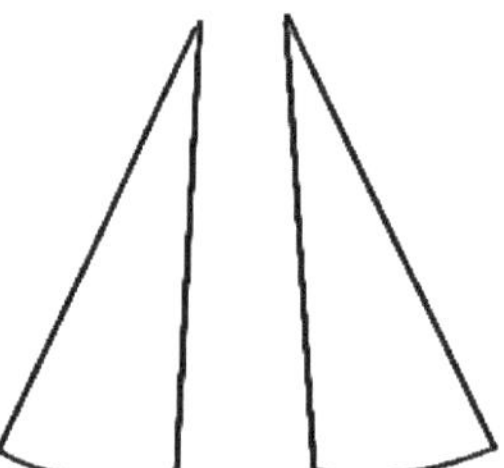

9. Arrange these seventeen sectors (one orange sector is divided into two parts) in alternate manner so that they form a rectangular shape as shown in fig.

half of circumference of circle

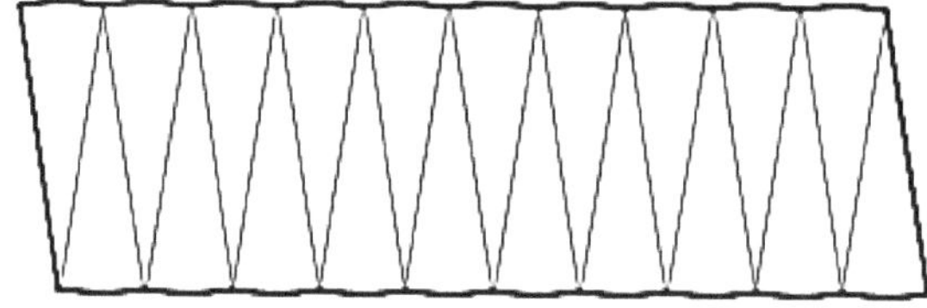

OBSERVATION

1. The area of the rectangular shape so formed with seventeen sectors is the same as the area of the circle.

   Length of the rectangular shape $= \frac{1}{2} \times$ circumference of circle $= \frac{1}{2} \times 2\pi r = \pi r$.
2. Breadth of the rectangular shape = radius of the circle

$\therefore$ Area of the rectangle $= L \times B = \pi r \times r = \pi r^2$ sq. units.

RESULT

Area of a circle with radius $r = \pi r^2$.

LEARNING OUTCOME

1. The figure formed by arranging 17 sectors of a circle is almost a rectangle.
2. As we increase the number of sectors of the circle, the figure of the rectangle becomes better and better.
3. Through this activity, students will learn to find the approximate result for the area of a circle.

ACTIVITY TIME

Find out the area of a circle of radius 6.3 cm by dividing the circle into 32 sectors.

VIVA-VOCE

Question 1. What shape will you obtain if you rotate a circle along diameter?
Answer: Sphere

Question 2. Define concentric circles.
Answer: Circles having the same Centre and different radii are called concentric circles.

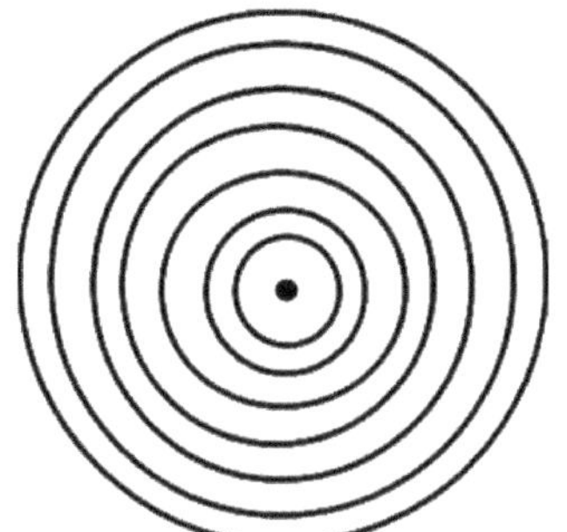

Question 3. What is the area of a circular ring?
Answer: $\pi(R^2 - r^2)$, where R = internal radius and r = internal radius of the ring.

Question 4. Define sector
Answer: It is the part of a circle between two radii and the corresponding arc.

MULTIPLE CHOICE QUESTION

Question 1.
What is the radius of the circle if the length of the arc is 22 cm and the central angle is 30°?
(a) 21cm.
(b) 24 cm.
(c) 42 cm.
(d) none of these

Question 2.
The area of a quadrant of a circle in the form of its diameter d is
(a) $\frac{\pi d^2}{8}$
(b) $\frac{\pi d^2}{16}$
(c) $\frac{\pi d^2}{4}$
(d) none of these

Question 3.
If a chord subtends a right angle at the Centre, then the area of the corresponding segment
(a) $\left(\frac{\pi}{4} - \frac{1}{2}\right) r^2$
(b) $\left(\frac{\pi}{4} + \frac{1}{2}\right)$
(c) $\left(\frac{1}{2} - \frac{\pi}{4}\right)$
(d) None of these

Question 4.
The perimeter of the sector of a circle of radius r is
(a) $\frac{\pi r\theta}{180°}$
(b) $\frac{\pi r\theta}{180°} + 2r$
(c) $\frac{2\pi r\theta}{360°} - 2r$
(d) none of these

Question 5.
Angle described by hour hand in 12 hours is
(a) 180°
(b) 720°
(c) 360°
(d) none of these

Answer Key

1.(c)	2.(b)	3.(a)	4.(b)	5.(c)

ACTIVITY 13

AREAS OF SECTORS FORMED AT THE VERTICES OF A TRIANGLE

OBJECTIVE

To verify that sum of areas of three sectors of the same radii 'r' formed at the vertices of any triangle are $\frac{1}{2}\pi r^2$ by paper cutting and pasting.

MATERIAL REQUIRED

Glazed paper, sketch pens, fevicol, a pair of scissors, a pencil, geometry box.

THEORY

1. Concept of different types of triangles.
2. Definition of a sector.
3. Area of circle $= \pi r^2$, r $\rightarrow$ radius.

PROCEDURE

1. Draw three different types of triangles on a glazed paper as shown in fig.
   (a) Equilateral ΔABC
   (b) Isosceles ΔPQR
   (c) Scalene ΔXYZ

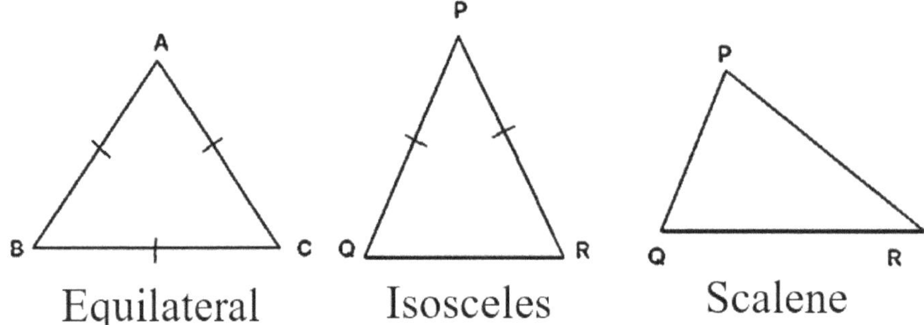

2. Cut an equilateral ΔABC as shown in fig.

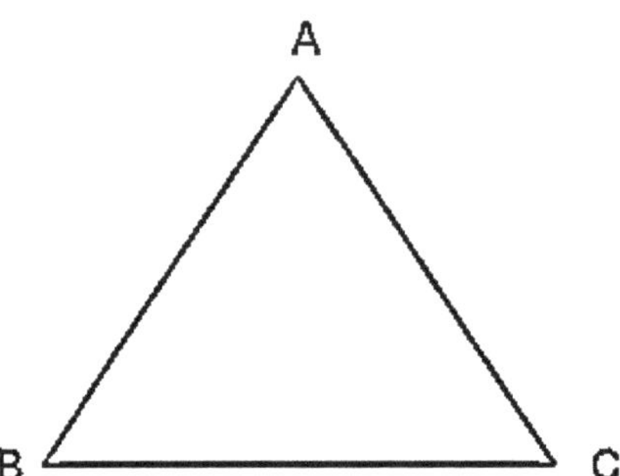

3. Taking vertices, A, B and C as centres of ΔABC, draw three sectors of same radii r.

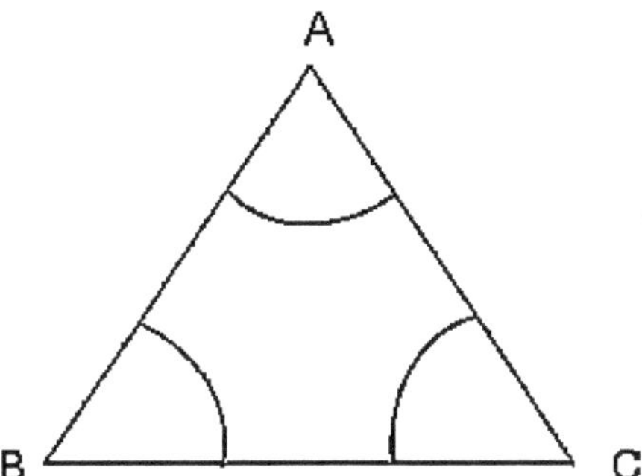

4. Cut these three sectors and marked them as 1,2,3 and fill different colours.

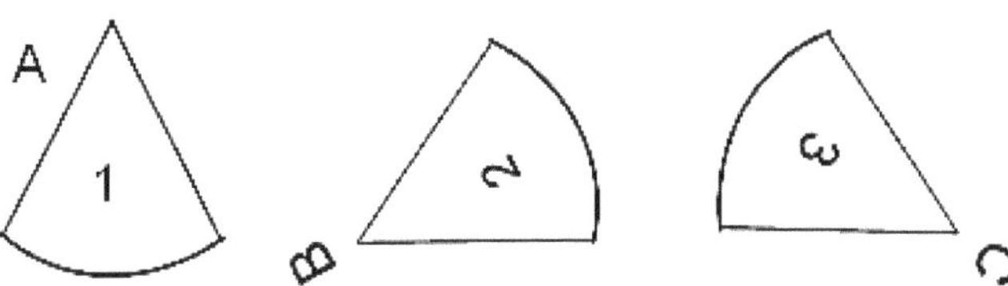

5. Draw a straight line and mark any point 'O' on it. Place three sectors 1,2,3 adjacent to each other so that the vertices A, B, C coincide with 'O' without leaving any gap as shown in fig.

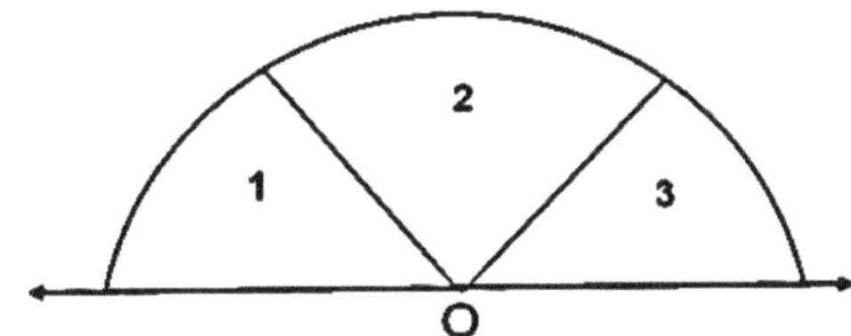

6. The same process (steps 1-5) can be taken up with the isosceles triangle and scalene triangle.

OBSERVATION

The shape formed on the straight line is a semi-circle

∴ area of circle $= \pi r^2$

∴ area of semicircle $= \frac{1}{2}\pi r^2$.

RESULT

It is verified that the sum of areas of three sectors of the same radii 'r' formed at the vertices of any triangle are $\frac{1}{2}\pi r^2$

LEARNING OUTCOME

The students can understand the concept of this activity through paper cutting. It is clear to them that a semicircle is always obtained, whatever be the type of a triangle.

ACTIVITY TIME

1. Find the sum of areas of four sectors of the same radii 'r' formed at the vertices (as Centre) of any quadrilateral through activity.

Hint:

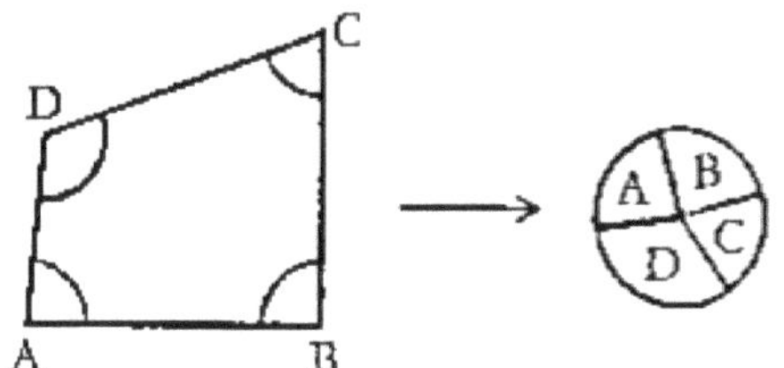

(Cut the sectors from vertices and arrange them as shown)

2. Find the sum of areas of five sectors of the same radii 'r' formed at the vertices (as Centre) of any pentagon through activity.

Hint:

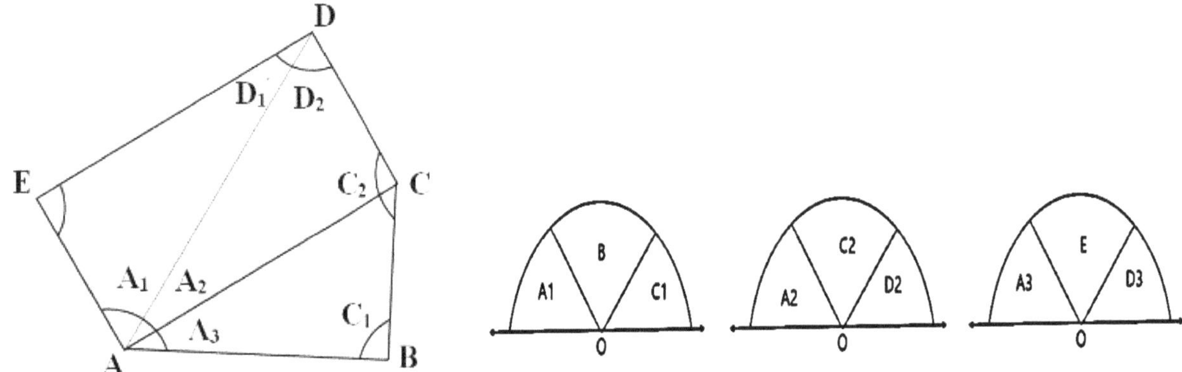

Question 1. What is the angle subtended by a circle at the Centre?
Answer: 360°.

Question 2. What is the sum of angles of four sectors of the same radii 'r' formed at the vertices (as Centre) at any quadrilateral?
Answer: 360°.

Question 3. If the perimeter of the semicircle is 12 cm, find its radius.
Answer: 7/3cm

Question 4. What is the area of a semicircle of radius 2 cm?
Answer: 2π.

Question 5. What is the difference between a sector and a segment of a circle?
Answer: A sector of a circle is formed by an arc and two radii of the circle, while a segment is one of its parts in which a chord divides a circle.

Question 6. Define chords.
Answer: A line segment joining two points on the circumference of a circle is known as a chord.

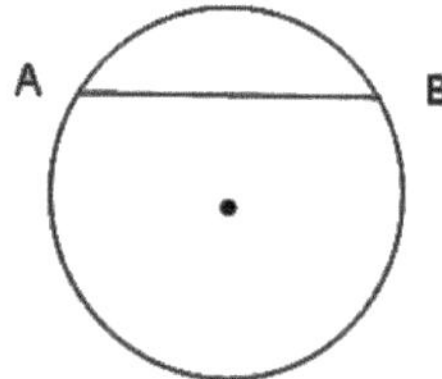

Question 7. Define a segment of a circle.
Answer: A chord divides a circle into two parts each of which is called a segment of a circle.

Question 8. "A tangent intersects the circle in more than one point". Is the statement true or false?
Answer: False

MULTIPLE CHOICE QUESTION

Question 1.
If the area of a semicircle is 121 cm^2, find its radius.
(a) $\sqrt{77}$cm
(b) $\sqrt{76}$cm
(c) $\sqrt{74}$cm
(d) None of these

Question 2.
If the perimeter and the area of a circle are numerically equal, then the radius of the circle is
(a) π units
(b) 2 units
(c) 4 units
(d) 5 units

Question 3.
The area of a sector of angle P (in degree) of a circle with radius R is
(a) $\frac{P}{180^\circ} \times 2\pi R^2$
(b) $\frac{P}{180^0} \times 2\pi R^2$
(c) $\frac{P}{360^0} \times 2\pi R^2$
(d) $\frac{P}{720^0} \times 2\pi R^2$

Question 4.
The area of the sector of a circle with a radius of 4 cm and angle of 30° is
(a) 4.91 cm
(b) 14.9 cm
(c) 4.19 cm
(d) 94.1cm

Question 5.
Find the area of a quadrant of the circle whose circumference is 22 cm.
(a) $\frac{77}{8}$ cm^2
(b) $\frac{76}{8}$ cm^2
(c) $\frac{77}{2}$ cm^2
(d) $\frac{77}{4}$ cm^2

Question 6.
Find the perimeter of the quadrant of a circle of radius 4.2 cm.
(a) 8.4 cm
(b) 12.6 cm
(c) 15 cm
(d) none of these

Question 7.
If the radius of a circle is increased by 100% by what percent of the area of the circle increases?
(a) 200%
(b) 300%
(c) 400%
(d) none of these

Question 8.
The perimeter of a sector with radius r and angle θ of a circle is given by
(a) $d + \frac{2\pi r\theta}{180^0}$
(b) $r + \frac{\pi r\theta}{180^0}$
(c) $\frac{\theta}{360^0} \times 2\pi r$
(d) $2r + \frac{\pi r\theta}{180^0}$

Question 9.
The area of the sector of a circle with a radius of 7 cm and angle of 120° is
(a) 51.33 cm^2
(b) 53.11 cm^2
(c) 53.13 cm^2
(d) none of these

Question 10.
The length of the minute hand of a clock is 14 cm. Find the area swept by the minute hand in 5 minutes.
(a) $\frac{145}{3}$ cm^2
(b) $\frac{514}{3}$ cm^2
(c) $\frac{451}{3}$ cm^2
(d) $\frac{154}{3}$ cm^2

Answer Key

1.(a)	2.(b)	3.(d)	4.(c)	5.(a)	6.(a)	7.(b)	8.(d)	9.(a)	10.(d)

ACTIVITY 14

RIGHT CIRCULAR CYLINDER

OBJECTIVE

To make a right circular cylinder of given height and circumference of the circular base from a given rectangle experimentally.

MATERIAL REQUIRED

Coloured papers, a pair of scissors, fevicol, cello tape, pencil, ruler.

THEORY

Formula for the circumference of a circle.

PROCEDURE

1. Draw and cut a rectangle of length = l and breadth = b from a coloured sheet of paper.
2. Curve the paper so that the two shorter sides come together.
3. Join the edges with cello tape.

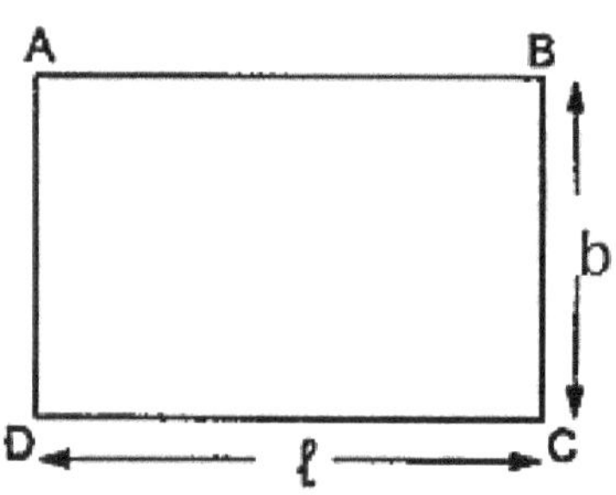

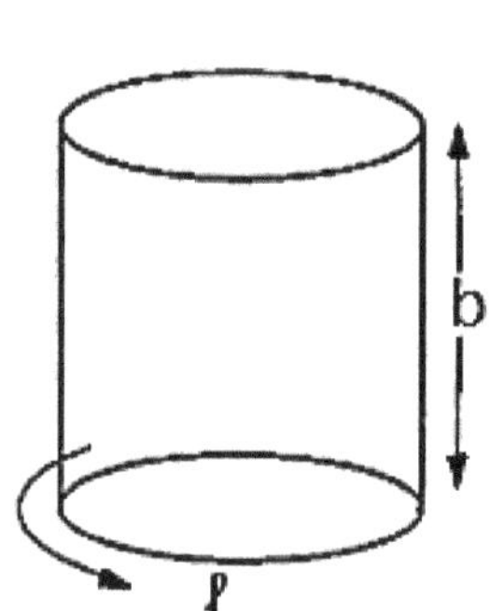

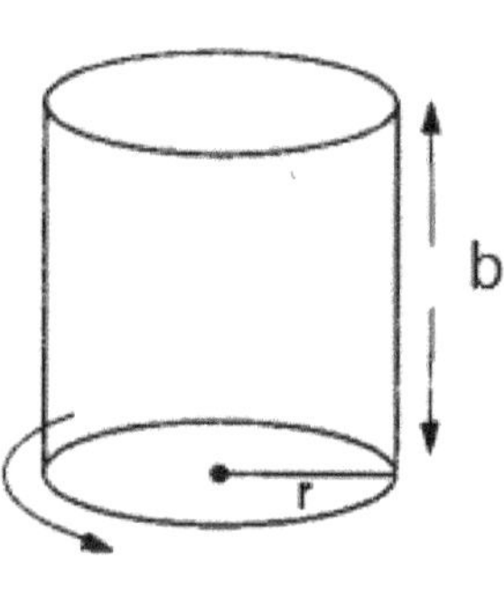

4. Write your observation.

OBSERVATION

1. Rectangle transforms into a cylinder. Let the radius of this cylinder be r.
2. Height of the cylinder = breath of rectangle, i.e., $\mathrm{b} = \mathrm{h}$.
3. Circumference of the base = length of the rectangle, i.e., $l = 2\pi r$.

RESULT

A right circular cylinder can be made of the height and circumference of the circularbase from the rectangle of desired length and breadth.

LEARNING OUTCOME

Students will learn to make a cylinder of the given height and circumference of the circular base. Circumference of base = length of the rectangular sheet

ACTIVITY TIME

Make a right circular cylinder of height 7 cm and circumference of base 20 cm.

VIVA-VOCE

Question 1. What is a cylinder?
Answer: On folding a rectangular sheet along the length or breadth, we get a shape called a cylinder.

Question 2. Is there any vertex of the cylinder?
Answer: No.

Question 3. What is the volume of a cylinder?
Answer: $\pi r^2 h$. Where r = radius of base, h = height of the cylinder.

Question 4. If the radius of the cylinder is doubled, then by how much its volume will increase?
Answer: Four times.

Question 5. If the radius of the base of a right circular cylinder is halved keeping the height the same, find the ratio of the volume of the reduced cylinder to that of the original cylinder.
Answer: $1:4$.

Question 6. If the height of a circular cylinder is reduced to one-ninth and the radius of its baseis tripled, then what will be the effect on the volume of the cylinder?
Answer: No change in the volume of the cylinder.

Question 7. If the height of the right circular cylinder is doubled then how much its volume will increase?
Answer: Two times.

Question 8. What is the axis of the cylinder?
Answer: The line joining the centres of the circular cross-sections of a cylinder is called the axis of the cylinder.

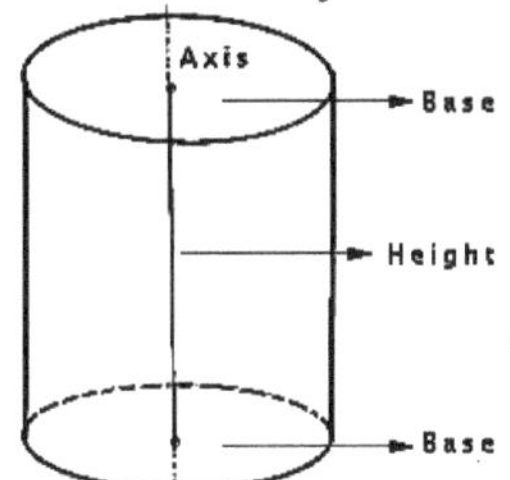

MULTIPLE CHOICE QUESTION

Question 1.
The volume of a cylinder with a radius of 12 cm and height of 28 cm is
(a) 12672 cm^3
(b) 16272 cm^3
(c) 12627 cm^3
(d) None of these

Question 2.
A cylindrical tank has a capacity of 6160 m. If the diameter of its base is 28 m, then its depth is
(a)12 m
(b) 10 m
(c) 8 m
(d) none of these

Question 3.
The curved surface area of a right circular cylinder is
(a) $\pi r^2 h$
(b) $2\pi rh$
(c) $2\pi r(h + r)$
(d) none of these

Question 4.
The circumference of the base of a cylindrical vessel is 132 cm and its height is 25 cm. How many litres of water can it hold?
(a) $3.465\ l$
(b) $34.65\ l$
(c) $346.5\ l$
(d) none of these

Question 5.
The radius and height of a cylinder are in the ratio 5: 7 and its volume are 550cm^3. Then its radius is.
(a) 7 cm
(b) 12 cm
(c) 5 cm
(d) none of these

Question 6.
The radii of two cylinders are in the ratio 2: 3 and their heights are in the ratio 5:4. Then the ratio of their volumes is l.
(a) 5: 9
(b) 5: 7
(c) 7: 9
(d) none of these

Question 7.
A metallic pipe is 77 cm long. The inner diameter of a cross-section is 4 cm, the outer diameter being 4.4 cm. Then its inner curved surface area is.
(a) 869 cm^2
(b) 968 cm^2
(c) 980 cm^2
(d) 960 cm^2

Question 8.
Find the depth of a cylindrical tank of radius 28 m, if its capacity is equal to that of a rectangular tank of size $28\text{ m} \times 16\text{ m} \times 11\text{ m}$.
(a) 2 m
(b) 3 m
(c) 4 m
(d) none of these

Question 9.
The diameter of a roller is 84 cm, and its length is 120 cm. It takes 500 complete revolutions to move once over to level the playground area of the playground in m is
(a) $1845\ m^2$
(b) $1854\ m^2$
(c) $1584\ m^2$
(d) none of these

Question 10.
The volume of a right circular cylinder which has a height of 21 cm, and a base radius of 5 cm is.
(a) 1650 cm^3
(b) 1056 cm^3
(c) 1605 cm^3
(d) 1560 cm^3

Answer Key

1.(a)	2.(b)	3.(b)	4.(b)	5.(c)	6.(a)	7.(b)	8.(a)	9.(c)	10.(a)

RIGHT CIRCULAR CONE

OBJECTIVE

To make a cone of given the slant height and the circumference of the circular base from the circular portion experimentally.

MATERIAL REQUIRED

Coloured chart papers, a pair of scissors, cello tape, geometry box.

THEORY

1. Circumference of the circle.
2. Concept of the sector of a circle.
3. Concept of Pythagoras theorem.

PROCEDURE

1. Draw and cut a circle from a coloured chart paper of radius equal to the given the slant height says l of the cone.

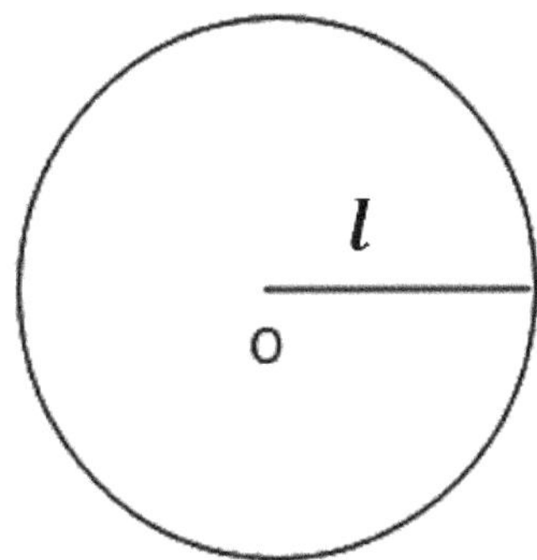

2. Mark a sector OAB such that major AB = circumference of the base of the cone. i.e., if r be the radius of the cone, then the length of major arc $AB = 2\pi r$.
3. Cut the sector AOB.
4. Fold the remaining paper by bringing the two radii OA and OB together.

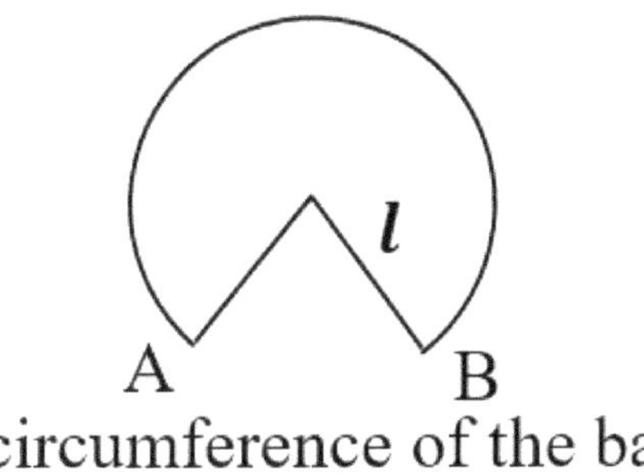

circumference of the base of the cone

OBSERVATION

When two radii are joined together, a cone is formed.

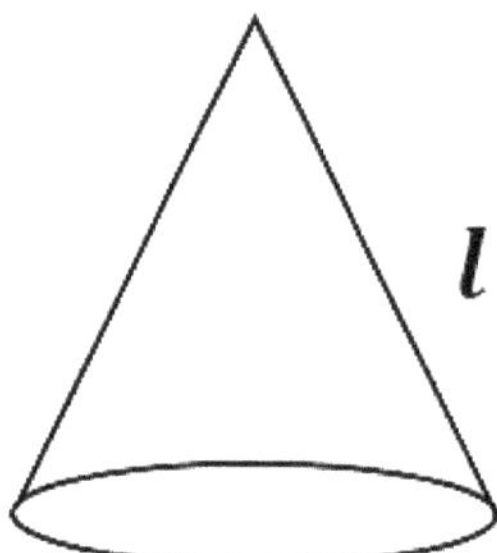

RESULT

A cone of a given the slant height and circumference of the base can be made experimentally.

LEARNING OUTCOME

Students will learn how to make a cone of a given slant height and circumference of the base from the sector of a circle. They will also learn how the radius of the circle becomes the slant height of the cone and the arc length of the circle becomes the circumference of the base of the cone.

ACTIVITY TIME

1. Find x.

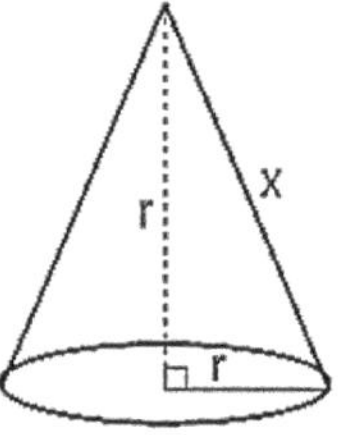

2. Find x.

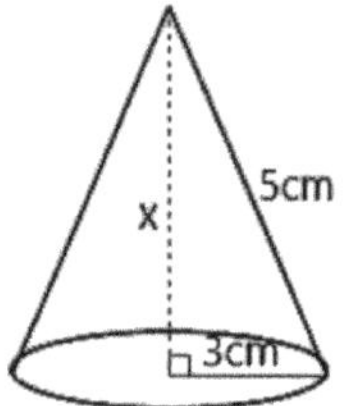

3. Find x.

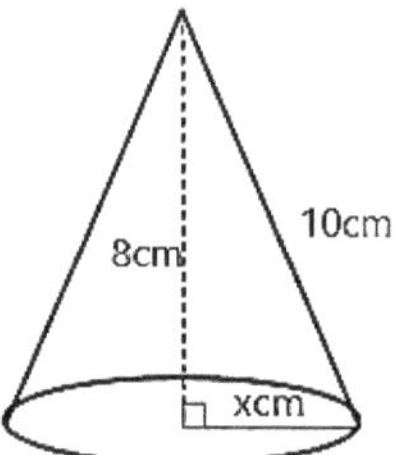

4. Make a right circular cone given the slant height of 13 cm and base radius of 5cm. Also, find its height by measurement and by calculation.

VIVA-VOCE

Question 1. How many vertices are there in a right circular cone?
Answer: One.

Question 2. What is the relation between the radius of the base, the height of the cone and the slant height of the cone?
Answer: $l^2 = r^2 + h^2$, where l = the slant height, r = radius, h = height.

Question 3. What are the different parts of a cone?
Answer: Circular base, vertex, curved surface.

Question 4. If the height of a cone is equal to the radius of the base of the cone, then find the slant height of the cone?
Answer: slant height = 2 × height of cone

Question 5. What is the slant height of a cone?
Answer: It is the distance of the vertex from any point on the base (circumference of the circle).

Question 6. What is the curved surface area of a cone?
Answer: πrl, where r = radius of the cone, l = the slant height of the cone.

Question 7. What is the volume of a cone?
Answer: $\frac{1}{3}\pi r^2 h$, where r = radius of cone and h = height of the cone.

Question 8. Give two examples of a right circular cone.
Answer: Birthday cap, cone of ice cream.

MULTIPLE CHOICE QUESTION

Question 1.
The radius of the base of a cone is 5 cm and the slant height are 13 cm. Then the height of the cone is
(a) 12 cm
(b) 8 cm
(c) 18 cm
(d) none of these

Question 2.
If the height of the cone is 6 cm and the radius of its base is 8 cm, then the slant height is
(a) 2 cm
(b) 10 cm
(c) 14 cm
(d) none of these

Question 3.
If the height and the slant height of a cone is 3 cm and 5 cm respectively, then theradius of its base is
(a) 2 cm
(b) 8 cm
(c) 4 cm
(d) none of these

Question 4.
Find the volume of a conical bucket as shown in fig.

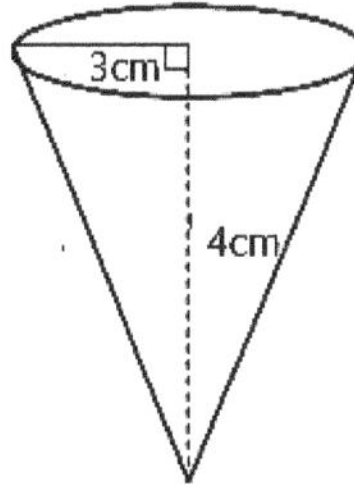

(a) 37.7 cm^3
(b) 37 cm^3
(c) 36.7 cm^3
(d) 36 cm^3

Question 5.
A conical pit of the top diameter of 3.5 m is 12 m deep. What is the capacity in kiloliter?
(a) 38.5 kl
(b) 3.85 kl
(c) 385 kl
(d) none of these

Question 6.

A right triangle ABC with sides 5 cm, 12 cm and 13 cm are revolved around the side 12 cm. What is the volume of the solid so obtained?

Take $\pi = 3.14$

(a) 314 cm^3 (c) 143 cm^3

(b) 341 cm^3 (d) none of these

Question 7.

Radius of the base of a cone is 3 cm and the slant height is 5 cm. The height of the coneis

(a) 3 cm (c) 5 cm

(b) 4 cm (d) 4.1 cm

Question 8.

Diameter of the base of a cone is 10.5 cm and its slant height is 10 cm. Its curved surface area is

(a) 165 cm^2 (c) 160 cm^2

(b) 156 cm^2 (d) 150 cm^2

Question 9.

Find the total surface area of a cone if its slant height is 21 m and the diameter of its base is 24 cm.

(a) 1244.57 m^2

(b) 1442.57 m^2

(c) 1440.57 m^2

(d) 1441.57 m^2

Question 10.

The volume of a cone of height 9 cm is 4871 cm^3. The diameter of its base is

(a) 8 cm

(b) 9 cm

(c) 4.5 cm

(d) none of these

Question 11.

What is the total surface area of a cone of radius 7 cm and height 24 cm?

(a) 710 cm^3 (c) 704 cm^3

(b) 700 cm^3 (d) 725 cm^3

Answer Key

1.(a)	2.(b)	3.(c)	4.(a)	5.(a)	6.(a)	7.(b)	8.(a)	9.(a)	10.(a)
11.(b)									

ACTIVITY 16 VOLUME OF A CYLINDER

OBJECTIVE
To get the formula for the volume of a right circular cylinder in terms of its height and base radius experimentally.

MATERIAL REQUIRED
Plastic clay, cutter, thermocol.

THEORY
1. Circumference of circle
2. Volume of cuboid

PROCEDURE
1. Make a cylinder of plastic clay of height say 'h' and base 'A circle of radius r.

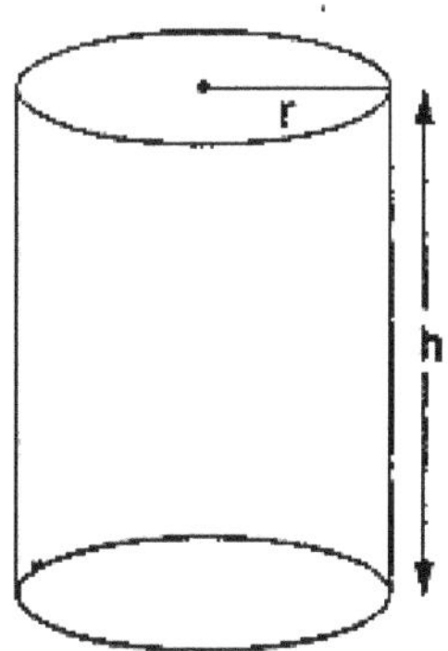

2. Cut the cylinder into 8 equal sectoral sections with the help of a cutter.

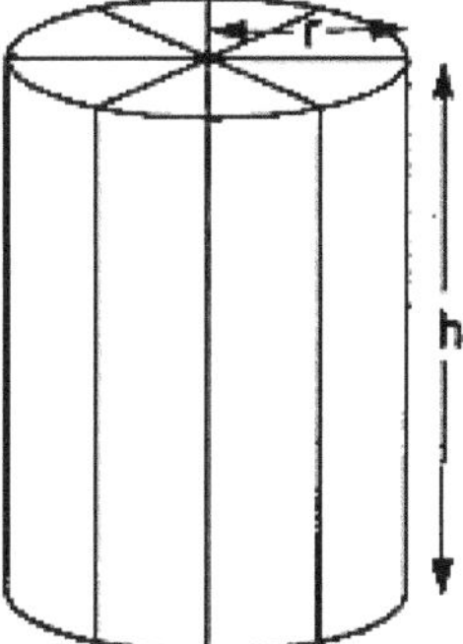

3. Place the sectoral segments alternatively to form a solid cuboid.

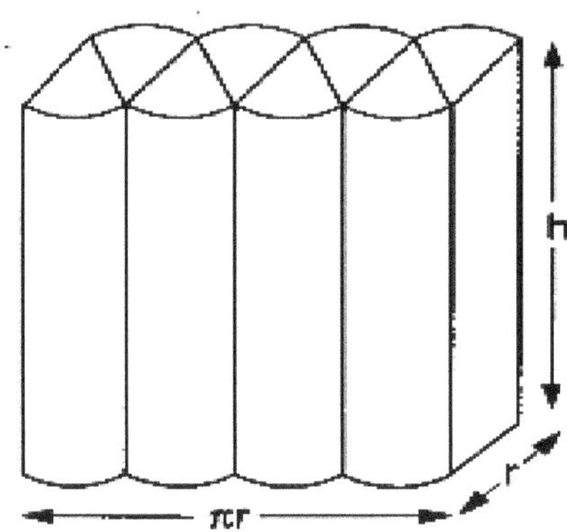

OBSERVATION

1. Combine cut out form a cuboid of height h and breadth r, i.e., the height of cuboid = height of the cylinder.
   breadth of cuboid = radius of the cylinder.
   The length of the cuboid $= \frac{1}{2}$ of the circumference of the base of the cylinder.
2. Volume of cuboid = Volume of cylinder $(V) = l \times b \times h = \frac{1}{2} \times 2\pi r \times r \times h = \pi r^2 h$

RESULT

Thus, the volume of cylinder is $\pi r^2 h$.

LEARNING OUTCOME

Students will learn how to get the formula for the volume of a cylinder with a given height and base radius experimentally.

ACTIVITY TIME

Make a cylinder of height 10 cm and radius 7 cm. Also, make a cone of the same height and same radius. Find the relation between their volumes.

VIVA-VOCE

Question 1. If the radius of the base of a right circular cylinder is halved, then by how much its volume will decrease?
Answer: One-fourth.

Question 2. If the radius of the base of the cylinder is doubled then the volume of this cylinder will be.
Answer: Four times.

Question 3. If the height of a circular cylinder is reduced to one-fourth and the radius of the base isdoubled, then what effect will be on the volume of the cylinder?
Answer: No effect.

Question 4. What is the volume of a right circular cylinder of height 21 cm and base radius 5 cm?
Answer: 1650 cm.

Question 5. Is the volume of a cylinder 3 times the volume of a cone of the same height and same diameter of the base?
Answer: Yes

Question 6. If r is radius and h be height, then the volume of a cylinder.
Answer: $\pi r^2 h$.

Question 7. If the radius of the base of a right circular cylinder is halved keeping the height the same,then what is the ratio of the volume of the reduced cylinder to that of the original cylinder?

Answer: 1:4

Question 8. The cylindrical cans have bases of the same size. One of the cans is 10 cm in height and the other is 20 cm in height. What is the ratio of their volumes?

Answer: 1:2

MULTIPLE CHOICE QUESTION

Question 1.

Inner diameter of a cylindrical wooden pipe is 24 cm, and its outer diameter is 28 cm.The length of the pipe is 35 cm. If 1cm^3 of wood has a mass of 0.6 g, then the mass of the pipe is

(a) 3.432 kg

(b) 34.32 kg

(c) 343.2 kg

(d) none of these

Question 2.

What is the capacity of a cylinder with a circular base of diameter 7 cm and height 10 cm?

(a) 384 cm^3

(b) 385 cm^3

(c) 386 cm^3

(d) none of these

Question 3.

Volume of a vessel in the form of a right circular cylinder is 1408cm^3 and its height is 7 cm. The radius of its base is

(a) 7 cm

(b) 9 cm

(c) 8 cm

(d) none of these

Question 4.

50 circular plates, each of radius 7 cm and thickness $\frac{1}{2}$ cm is placed one aboveanother to form a solid right circular cylinder. Then the volume of the cylinder is

(a) 3850 cm^3

(b) 3805 cm^3

(c) 3085 cm^3

(d) none of these

Question 5.

If the diameter of the cross-section of a wire is decreased by 5%, how much percent will its length be increased so that the volume remains same?

(a) 10.8%

(b) 1.08%

(c) 18.0%

(d) 1.80%

Question 6.

A rectangular sheet of paper 44 cm × 18 cm is rolled along its length and a cylinder is formed. Find the volume of the cylinder.

(a) 2772 cm^3

(b) 2727 cm^3

(c) 7272 cm^3

(d) 7722 cm^3

Question 7.

Water is being pumped out through a cylindrical pipe whose internal diameter is 7 cm. If the flow of water is 72 cm per second, how many litres of water is being pumped out in one hour?

(a) 9979.2 l

(b) 9199.2 l

(c) 7999.2 l

(d) 2999.2 l

Question 8.

A patient in a hospital is given soup daily in a cylindrical bowl of diameter 7 cm. If the bowl is filled with soup up to a height of 4 cm, how much soup the hospital has to prepare daily for 250 patients?

(a) 38.5 l

(b) 35.8 l

(c) 58.3 l

(d) 3.85 l

Question 9.
If the lateral surface area of a cylinder is 94.2 cm^2 and its height is 5cm, then the volume of the cylinder is
(a) $130.41\ \text{cm}^3$
(b) $141.30\ \text{cm}^3$
(c) 114.03cm^3
(d) none of these

Question 10.
Volume of a cone of base radius 3 cm and height 7 cm is 66cm^3. The volume of a cylinder with the same base and height is
(a) $198\ \text{cm}^3$
(b) $189\ \text{cm}^3$
(c) $819\ \text{cm}^3$
(d) none of these

Answer Key

1.(a)	2.(b)	3.(c)	4.(a)	5.(a)	6.(a)	7.(a)	8.(a)	9.(b)	10.(a)

ACTIVITY 17

VOLUME OF A CONE

OBJECTIVE
To get the formula for the volume of a right circular cone experimentally.

MATERIAL REQUIRED
One cone and one cylinder have the same height and base radius, sand.

THEORY
1. Formula for the volume of a cylinder.
2. Concept of volume and its proportionality to the quantity of matter.

PROCEDURE
1. Fill the cone with sand.
2. Pour the sand from the cone into the cylinder.
3. Fill the cone with sand again and pour it to the cylinder.
4. Repeat the same process until the cylinder fills completely with sand.

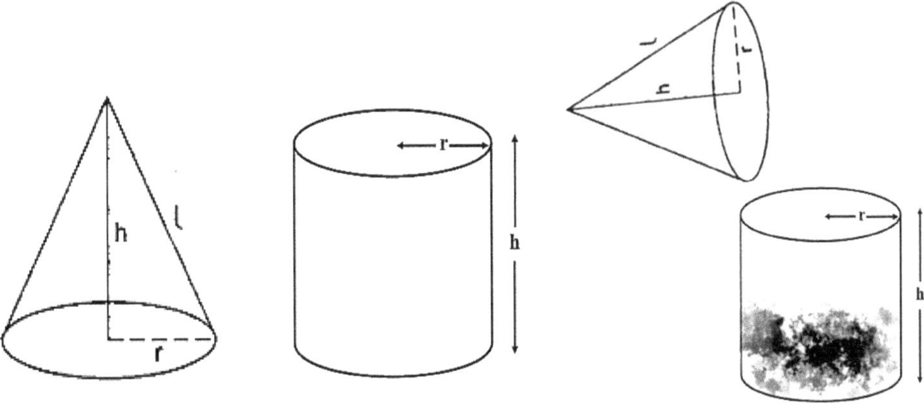

OBSERVATION AND RESULT
Students will observe that the cylinder gets filled after pouring the sand three times from the cone.

Volume of cone $= \frac{1}{3}$ Volume of cylinder $= \frac{1}{3}\pi r^2 h$

LEARNING OUTCOME
Through this experiment, students will learn the relationship between the volume of a cone and a cylinder.

ACTIVITY TIME
1. Find the volume of the cone.
2. What will be the volume of the cylinder having the same height and radiusgiven above?

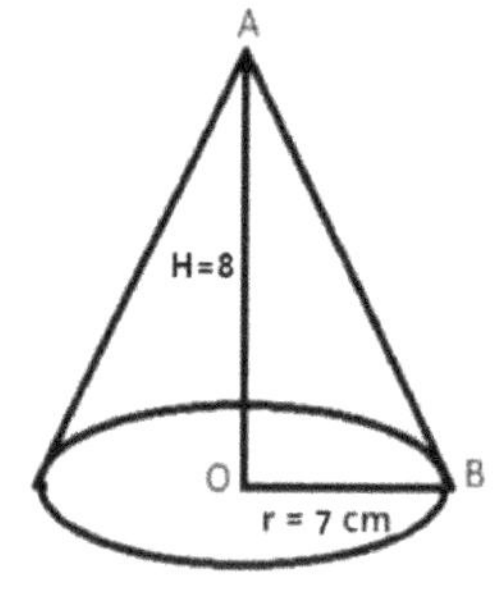

VIVA-VOCE

Question 1. Radius of a cone is halved, and height is doubled. What effect will be on its volume?
Answer: It will be half of original

Question 2. Radii of two cones of the same heights are in the ratio 2:5. Find the ratio of their volume.
Answer: 4: 25.

Question 3. What is the volume of a cone?
Answer: $\frac{1}{3}\pi r^2 h$

Question 4. Two cones have their heights in the ratio 1:3 and the radii of their bases are in the ratio 3:1. What is the ratio of their volumes?
Answer: 3: 1.

Question 5. Base radii of two cones of the same heights are in the ratio 3:5. Find the ratio of theirvolumes?
Answer: 9: 25.

Question 6. What is the ratio of the volume of a cylinder to the volume of a cone of the same height andthe same base?
Answer. 3: 1.

Question 7. Ratio of volumes of two cones having, the same base radius is 9:25, then what is the ratio of their heights?
Answer: 9: 25.

Question 8. Can we say that volume of a cone is 3 times the volume of a cylinder?
Answer: No.

MULTIPLE CHOICE QUESTION

Question 1.
The height of a cone is 15 cm. If its volume is $1571.4 cm^3$. Then the radius of the base is
(a) 10 cm
(b) 15 cm
(c) 5 cm
(d) none of these

Question 2.
Volume of the right circular cone with radius 3.5 cm, height 12 cm is
(a) $145 cm^3$
(b) $154 cm^3$
(c) $541 cm^3$
(d) none of these

Question 3.
The volume of the largest right circular cone that can be fit in a cube whose edge is 14 cm, is
(a) $71.86 cm^3$
(b) $718.6 cm^3$
(c) $718.6 cm^3$
(d) none of these

Question 4.
The radius and height of right circular cone are in the ratio 5 :12. If its volume is 2512 cm^3. Then the slant height is
(a) 10 cm
(b) 24 cm
(c) 26 cm
(d) none of these

Question 5.
A heap of wheat is in the form of a cone whose diameter is 10.5 m and height are 3 m, then the volume is
(a) 86.625 m^3
(b) 8.6625 m^3
(c) 866.25 m^3
(d) none of these

Question 6.
A semi-circular thin sheet of metal of diameter 28 cm is bent to make an open conical cup. Then the capacity of the cup is
(a) 622.36 cm^3
(b) 62.236 cm^3
(c) 6223.6 cm^3
(d) none of these

Question 7.
Volume of a cone of base radius 6 cm is 264 cm'. There its height is
(a) 5 cm
(b) 6 cm
(c) 7 cm
(d) none of these

Question 8.
Volume of a cone of height 12 cm is 154 cm. Then the diameter of the base is
(a) 3.5 cm
(b) 7 cm
(c) 3.4 cm
(d) 7.1 cm

Question 9.
The volume of a right circular cone with a radius 6 cm and height 7 cm is
(a) 246 cm
(b) 264 cm
(c) 462 cm
(d) none of these

Question 10.
The volume of a cone is 1540 cm. If the radius of its base is 10 cm, then the height of the cone is
(a) 147 cm
(b) 14.8 cm
(c) 14.7 cm
(d) 1.47 cm

Answer Key

1.(a)	2.(b)	3.(c)	4.(d)	5.(a)	6.(d)	7.(c)	8.(b)	9.(b)	10.(c)

SURFACE AREA OF A CYLINDER

OBJECTIVE
To find the curved surface area and total surface area of a cylinder experimentally.

MATERIAL REQUIRED
A white chart paper, a cylinder made of paper, a pair of scissors, a ruler, fevicol.

THEORY
1. Area of a rectangle.
2. Area of a circle.
3. Concept of the surface area of a cylinder.

PROCEDURE
1. Remove the top and bottom circles of the cylinder.
2. Make a vertical cut in the curved surface and lay the cylinder flat to get a rectangle as shown.

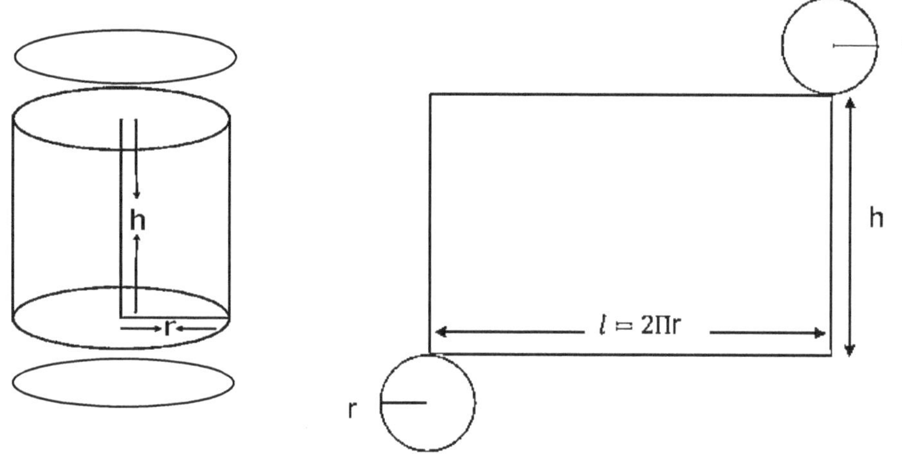

3. Measure the length and breadth of the rectangle so formed.

OBSERVATION
1. Top and bottom of cylinders are circles.
   Therefore, Area of 2 circles = πr^2, where **r** is the radius of the base circle of the cylinder
2. Length of rectangle =circumference of the base of cylinder =2πr
3. Breadth of rectangle =height =h
4. Area of rectangle = $\pi r \times h$ =curved surface area of the cylinder
5. Total surface area of cylinder = $2\pi rh + \pi r^2$
   $= 2\pi r(h + r)$

RESULT
Curved surface area of a cylinder = $2\pi rh$
Total surface area of a cylinder = $2\pi r(h + r)$

LEARNING OUTCOME
This activity clears the concept of curved surface area (lateral surface area) and the total surface area of a cylinder.

ACTIVITY TIME

Calculate the total surface area in terms of radius, where 'd represents the diameterof the cylinder.

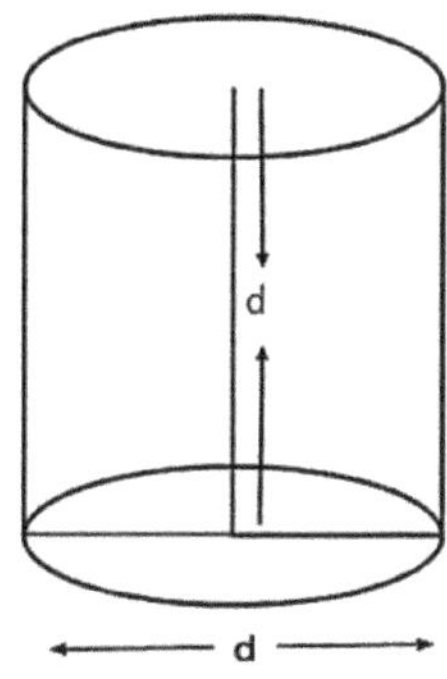

VIVA-VOCE

Question 1. What is the curved surface area of a cylinder?
Answer: $2\pi rh$.

Question 2. What is the total surface area of a cylinder?
Answer: $2\pi r(h + r)$.

Question 3. Write the number of circular faces of a cylinder?
Answer: 2

Question 4. What is the area of the circular face of the cylinder?
Answer: πr^2.

Question 5. If $h = 7cm$ and $r = 2cm$, find the lateral surface area of a cylinder.
Answer: $2\pi rh = 2 \times \frac{22}{7} \times 2 \times 7 = 88 \text{ cm}^3$

Question 6. What is the total area of circular faces of a cylinder?
Answer: $2\pi r^2$.

Question 7. What will be the curved surface area of a cylinder if its height is 3 times its radius?
Answer: $6\pi r^2$.

Question 8. What will be the curved surface area of a cylinder if its height is equal to the diameter of the base?
Answer: $4\pi r^2$.

Question 9. A cylinder has a curved surface area of 2640 cm^2 and radius of 14 cm, what is the height of cylinder?
Answer: 30 cm

MULTIPLE CHOICE QUESTION

Question 1.
The curved surface area of a right circular cylinder of height 14 cm is 88 cm^2. The diameter of the base of
the cylinder is
(a) 2 cm
(b) 1 cm
(c) 1.5 cm
(d) none of these

Question 2.
The curved surface area of a right circular cylinder is 4.4 m^2. If the radius of the base of the cylinder is
0.7 m, find its height.
(a) 2 m
(b) 1.5 m
(c) 1 m
(d) none of these

Question 3.
A cylindrical pillar is 5 m in diameter and 3.5 m in height. Find the cost of painting the curved surface of the pillar at the rate of Rs.12.50/ m^2
(a) Rs. 69.75
(b) Rs. 687.5
(c) Rs. 67.75
(d) none of these

Question 4.
A rectangular sheet of paper 44 cm × 18 cm is rolled along its length and a cylinderis formed. The radius of the cylinder is
(a) 7 cm
(b) 9 cm
(c) 22 cm
(d) none of these

Question 5.
The radius and height of a cylinder are in the ratio $5:7$ and its curved surface area is $220\ cm^2$. The radius and height are respectively
(a) 5 cm and 7 cm
(b) 7 cm and 5 cm
(c) 5 cm and 5 cm
(d) 1 cm and 7 cm

Question 6.
The curved surface area of a cylinder is 1000 cm^2 and its diameter is 20 cm. The height of the cylinder is
(a) 15.9 cm
(b) 15.8 cm
(c) 19.5 cm
(d) none of these

Question 7.
Find the curved surface area of a right circular cylinder of height 14 cm and base radius 1 cm.
(a) $88\ cm^2$
(b) $80\ cm^2$
(c) $82\ cm^2$
(d) $84\ cm^2$

Question 8.
What is the height of a cylinder of base radius as 1 cm and curved surface area as 88 cm2?
(a) 11 cm
(b) 14 cm
(c) 44 cm
(d) none of these

Question 9.
A metal pipe is 77 cm long. The inner diameter of a cross-section is 4 cm, the outer diameter being 4.4 cm. Its outer curved surface area is
(a) $1064.8cm^2$
(b) $1406.8cm^2$
(c) $1460.8cm^2$
(d) none of these

Question 10.
What is the curved surface area of a right circular cylinder of base radius 0.7 m and height 1 m?
(a) $4.4\ m^2$
(b) $4.1\ m^2$
(c) $1.1m^2$
(d) none of these

Answer Key

1.(a)	2.(c)	3.(b)	4.(a)	5.(a)	6.(a)	7.(a)	8.(b)	9.(a)	10.(a)

ACTIVITY 19

SURFACE AREA OF A CONE

OBJECTIVE
To find the formula for the lateral surface area and total surface area of a right circular cone experimentally.

MATERIAL REQUIRED
A cone made of chart paper, a pair of scissors, geometry box, fevicol, cello tape.

THEORY
1. Area of circle $= \pi r^2$
2. Area of parallelogram $= b \times h$ (b = base, h = height).
3. Circumference of circle $= 2\pi r$

PROCEDURE
1. Make a cone of pink chart paper having base radius r, the slant height 'l' and height h.
2. Cut the cone along with the slant height as shown in fig as per the dotted line and unroll it

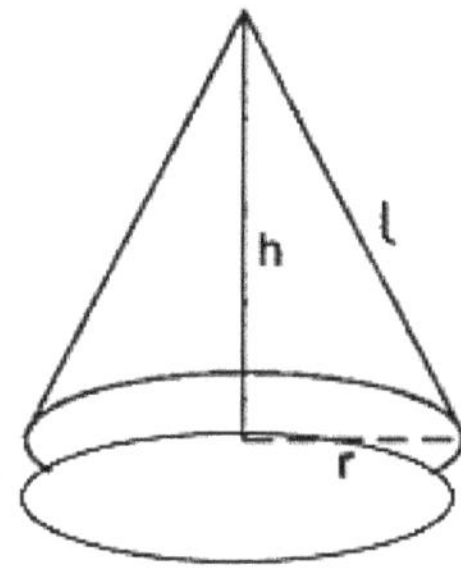

   to get a sector, as shown in fig(ii). Name this sector OAB.
3. Identify the arc length AB of the sector OAB = circumference of the base of the cone. radius of the sector OAB = the slant height of the cone. As shown in fig(ii).
4. Cut the sector OAB into 4 small equal sectors, along dotted lines as shown in fig(ii) and fill red colour in two sectors as shown.
5. Arrange these small sectors to get a parallelogram as shown in fig(iii)

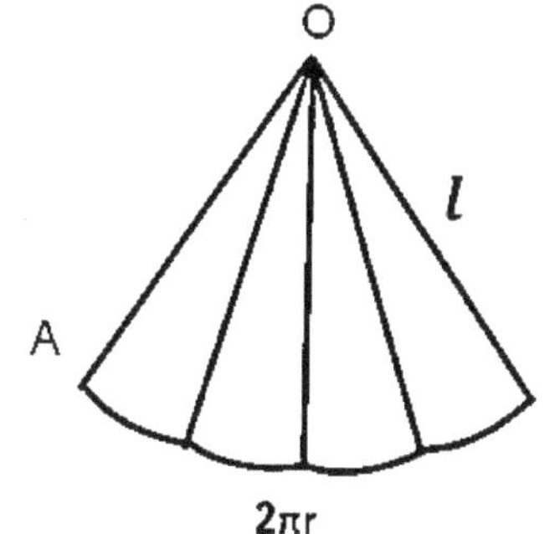

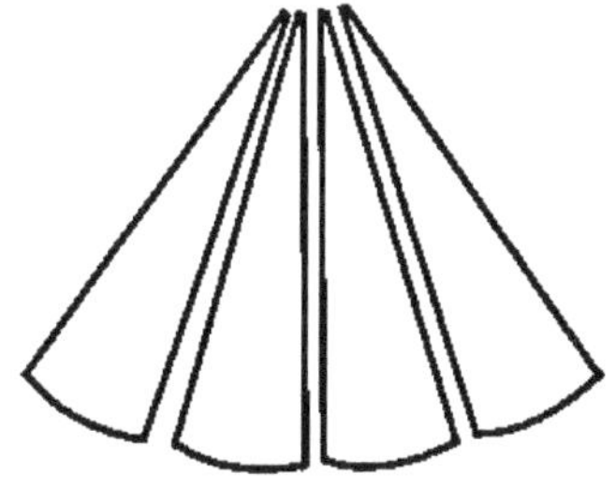

fig(ii)

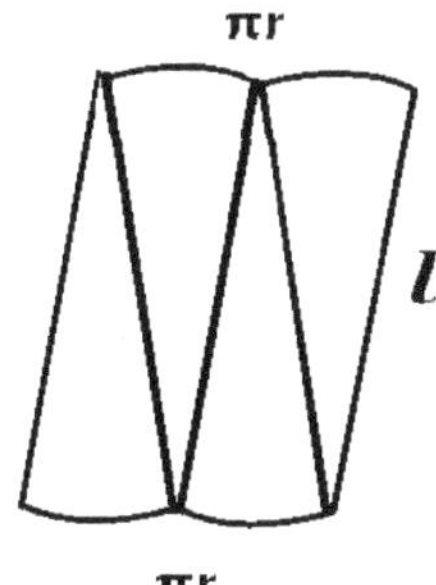

fig(iii)

OBSERVATION

1. Base of parallelogram $= \frac{1}{2} \times$ length of sector OAB $= \frac{1}{2} \times 2\pi r = \pi r$
2. Altitude of parallelogram the slant height of cone $= l$
3. Area of parallelogram $= \pi r \times l =$ Curved surface area of cone.
4. Total surface area of cone $= \pi r l +$ area of the circular base of cone
$= \pi r l + \pi r^2$
$= \pi r(l + r)$

LEARNING OUTCOME

Students will learn the concept to differentiate between the curved surface area and total surface area of a cone.

ACTIVITY TIME

1. Find the lateral surface area of a cone in the figure given.
2. Find the total surface area of a cone in the figure given.

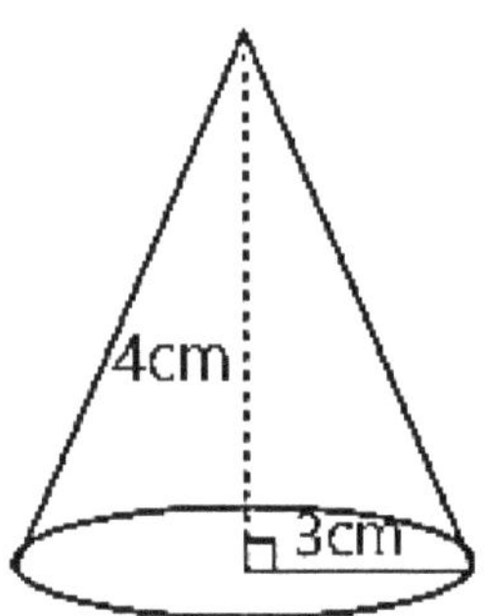

VIVA-VOCE

Question 1. What is the relation between the slant height and base radius of a cone?
Answer: $l^2 = h^2 + r^2$, l = the slant height,
r— radius of the cone, h = height of the cone.

Question 2. What is the lateral surface area of a cone?
Answer: πrl. l = the slant height, r— radius of base.

Question 3. What is the total surface area of a cone?
Answer: $\pi r(l + r)$, l=the slant height,
r = radius of base.

Question 4. What is the lateral surface area of a cone if its height is 2 times the radius?
Answer: $\sqrt{5}\pi r^2$

Question 5. How many circular faces are there in a solid cone?
Answer: One.

Question 6. Number of vertex of a cone is
Answer: One.

Question 7. Find the slant height of a cone of base radius 3 cm and height 4 cm.
Answer: 5 cm.

Question 8. What is the radius of the base of a cone of height 6 cm and the slant height 10 cm?
Answer: 8 cm.

Question 9. Number of base of a cone is?
Answer: One.

MULTIPLE CHOICE QUESTION

Question 1.
Diameter of the base of a cone is 10.5 cm and its slant height is 10 cm. Its curved surface area is
(a) 163 cm^2
(b) 165 cm^2
(c) 156 cm^2
(d) none of these

Question 2.
Curved surface area of a cone is 308 cm^2 and its slant height is 14 cm. Radius of the base is
(a) 7 cm
(b) 14 cm
(c) 22 cm
(d) none of these

Question 3.
A Joker's cap is in the form of a right circular cone of base radius 7 cm and height 24 cm. Find the area of the sheet required to make 10 such caps.
(a) 5500 cm^2
(b) 5050 cm^2
(c) 5005 cm^2
(d) none of these

Question 4.
The height of a cone is 16 cm, and its base radius is 12 cm. Find its curved surface area.
(a) 753.16 cm^2
(b) 753.6 cm^2
(c) 753.61cm^2
(d) none of these

Question 5.
The radius and height of a cone are in the ratio $4:3$. The area of the base is 154 cm^2. What is the area of its curved surface?
(a) 129.5 cm^2
(b) 195.2 cm^2
(c) 192.5 cm^2
(d) none of these

Question 6.
The radius and the slant height of a cone are in the ratio $4:7$. If its curved surface area is 792 cm^2. Find its radius.
(a) 12 cm
(b) 11 cm
(c) 13 cm
(d) 10 cm

Question 7.
Curved surface area of a cone of base radius 7 cm is 308 cm^2, then the slant height is
(a) 7 cm
(b) 14 cm
(c) 21 cm
(d) 28 cm

Question 8.
Total surface area of a cone of base radius 7cm is 462 cm^2, then the slant height is
(a) 14 cm
(b) 28 cm
(c) 12 cm
(d) none of these

Question 9.
A conical tent is 10 m high, and the radius of its base is 24 m, then its the slant height
(a) 24 m
(b) 25 m
(c) 26 m
(d) none of these

Question 10.
Curved surface area of a cone of base radius 7 m and the slant height of 25 m is
(a) 550 m^2
(b) 505 m^2
(c) 555 m^2
(d) none of these

Answer Key

1.(b)	2.(a)	3.(a)	4.(b)	5.(c)	6.(a)	7.(b)	8.(a)	9.(c)	10.(a)

ACTIVITY 20 COMPARISON OF CURVED SURFACE AREAS AND TOTAL SURFACE AREAS OF TWO RIGHT CIRCULAR CYLINDERS

OBJECTIVE

To compare the curved surface areas and total surface areas of two right circular cylinders which are formed from rectangular sheets of paper with the same dimensions.

MATERIAL REQUIRED

Coloured glazed paper, sketch pens, a pair of scissors, fevicol, cello tape, geometrybox.

THEORY

1. Construction of a cylinder from the rectangular sheet by paper folding.
2. Area of rectangle = length × breadth
3. Circumference and area of a circle
   $C = 2\pi r, A = \pi r^2$

PROCEDURE

1. Take two rectangular sheets of paper of the same dimensions as $l = 14$ cm and $b = 7$cm named as rectangle 1 and rectangle 2.

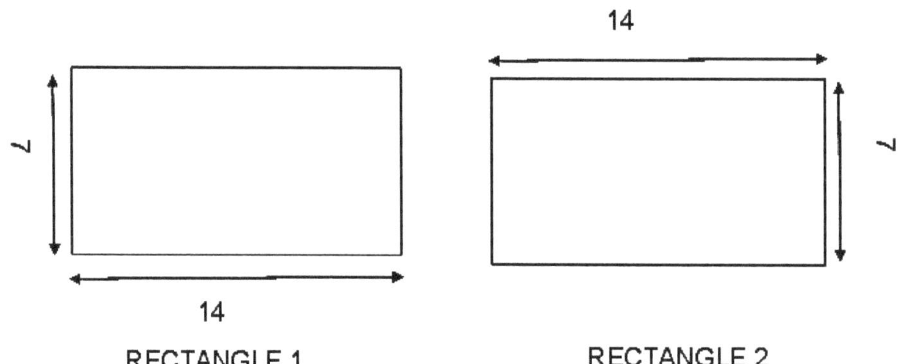

2. Curve the rectangle 1 along its length l =14 cm.
3. Join two ends with cello tape to get a cylinder.

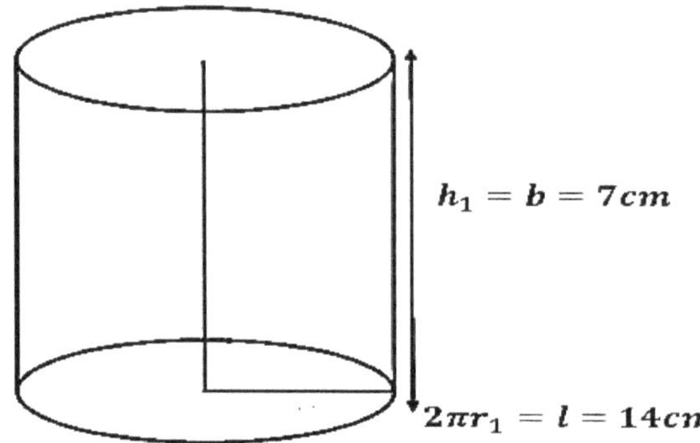

4. Similarly, curve rectangle 2 along its breadth b =7 cm to get another cylinderas shown in the figure.

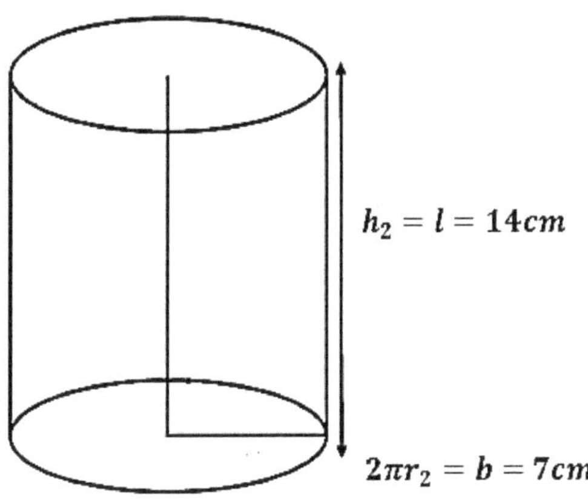

OBSERVATION FOR RECTANGLE 1:

length of the rectangle $=$ circumference of the circular base of the cylinder

$$= 2\pi r_1 = l = 14\text{cm}$$

$$= r_1 = \frac{14}{2\pi} = \frac{7}{\pi}$$

breadth of the rectangle = height of the cylinder

$$b = h_1 = 7 \text{ cm.}$$

curved surface area $C_1 = 2\pi r_1 h_1$

Total surface area $T_1 = 2\pi r_1^2 + C_1 = 2\pi \times \frac{49}{\pi^2} + 98 = 98\left(\frac{1+\pi}{\pi}\right)$

For rectangle 2:

breadth of the rectangle = circumference of the circular base of the cylinder

$$= 2\pi r_2 = b = 7\text{cm}$$

$$= r_2 = \frac{7}{2\pi}$$

length of the rectangle = height of the cylinder

$$h_2 = l = 14\text{cm}$$

curved surface area $C_2 = 2\pi r_2 h_2$

Total surface area $T_2 = 2\pi r_2^2 + C_2 = 2\pi \times \frac{49}{4\pi^2} + 98 = 49\left(\frac{1}{2\pi} + 2\right) = 49\left(\frac{1+4\pi}{\pi}\right)$

RESULT

1. The curved surface areas (or lateral surface areas) of two cylinders of different heights and radius formed from the two rectangular sheets of paper of the same dimensions are the same.
2. The total surface areas of two cylinders of different heights and radius formed from the two rectangular sheets of paper of the same dimensions are not same.

LEARNING OUTCOME

The concept of comparison of curved surface area and total surface area of two cylinders formed from the two rectangular sheets of paper of same dimension isclearer. Students can easily understand that

$C_1 = C_2$ but $T_1 \mp T_2$

ACTIVITY TIME

Take a rectangular sheet of paper of size $22 \text{ cm} \times 10 \text{ cm}$. Form two cylinders.

(i) curved along its length

(ii) curved along with its breadth.

Compare the lateral surface areas and total surface areas of these two cylinders.

VIVA-VOCE

Question 1. Find the height of a right circular cylinder made from a rectangle of length 15 cm and breadth 12 cm. It is curved along its length.
Answer: 12 cm.

Question 2. What is the curved surface area of a cylinder obtained from a square of side 5 cm?
Answer: $25\ \text{cm}^2$.

Question 3. Radius of the base of a paper cylinder is 7 cm and it is cut along its height. Find the length of the paper obtained.
Answer: $l = \text{circumference of base} = 2\pi r = 2 \times \frac{22}{7} \times 7 = 44\text{cm}$.

MULTIPLE CHOICE QUESTION

Question 1.
If the circumference of a circular base of a cylinder of height 2 cm is 132 cm, thenthe radius of the base is

(a) 21 cm
(b) 42 cm
(c) $\frac{21}{2}\ cm$
(d) none of these

Question 2.
A rectangular sheet of paper $44\text{cm} \times 18$ cm is rolled along its length and a cylinder is formed. What will be the height of the cylinder?

(a) 44 cm
(b) 18 cm
(c) 22 cm
(d) 9 cm

Question 3.
The area of a rectangular paper is 88 cm. Find its length if we obtain a circular cylinder of height 14 cm from it. [Hint: $27\pi rh$ = area of a rectangle]

(a) 44cm
(b) 88cm
(c) 88cm
(d) none of these

Question 4.
The diameter of a roller is 1.4 m, and it is 2 m long. How much area will it cover in 2 revolutions?

(a) $17.6\ \text{m}^2$
(b) $16.7\ \text{m}^2$
(c) 61.7m^2
(d) none of these

Question 5.
The area of a circular base of a cylinder is πcm^2 and its height is 5 cm. Find the lateral surface area and the total surface area of the cylinder.

(a) $8\pi\text{cm}^2, 10\pi\text{cm}^2$
(b) $10\pi\text{cm}^2, 12\pi\text{cm}^2$
(c) $10\pi\text{cm}^2, 10\pi\text{cm}^2$
(d) none of these

Answer Key

1.(a)	2.(b)	3.(c)	4.(a)	5.(b)

ACTIVITY 21 COMPARISON OF VOLUMES OF TWO RIGHT CIRCULAR CYLINDERS

OBJECTIVE

To compare the volumes of two right circular cylinders which are formed from two rectangular sheets of paper with same dimensions.

MATERIAL REQUIRED

Coloured glaze paper, a pair of scissors, cello tape, geometry box, fevicol.

THEORY

1. To make a cylinder from a rectangular sheet.
2. Circumference of circle $= 2\pi r$ and area of circle $= \pi r^2$ where r is the radius of the circle.
3. Volume of right circular cylinder $= \pi r^2 h$ (r- radius of circular base and h is the height of the cylinder)

PROCEDURE

1. Cut two rectangles of the same dimensions a $l = 22\text{cm}$ and $b = 10$ cm.
2. Name them as rectangle 1 and rectangle 2.

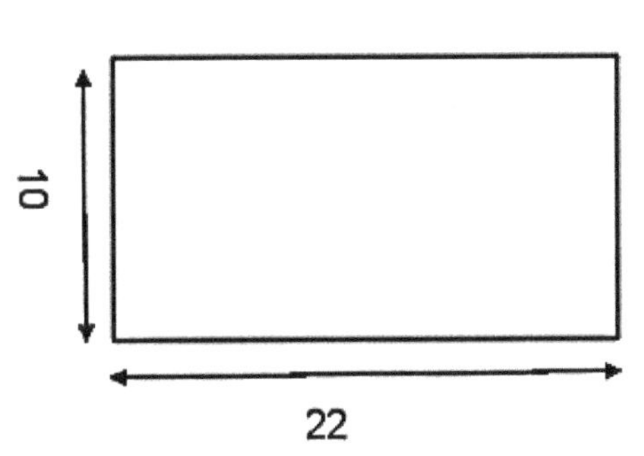

RECTANGLE 1

22

10

RECTANGLE 2

3. Curve rectangle 1 along its length and join the ends with cello tape to get acylinder.

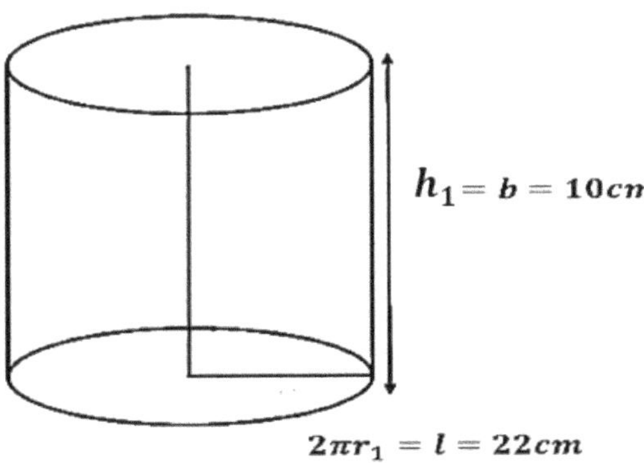

4. Curve rectangle 2 along with its breadth and join the ends with cello tape to get another cylinder.

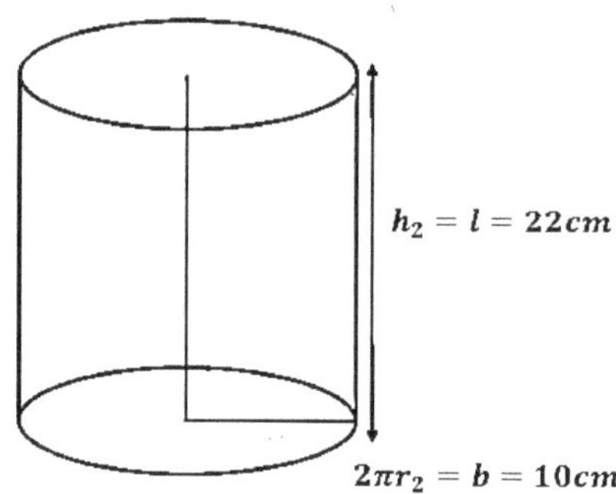

OBSERVATION FOR RECTANGLE 1:

length of the rectangle = circumference of the circular base of the cylinder

$= 2\pi r_1 = 22\text{cm}.$

$= r_1 = \frac{11}{\pi}$

breadth of the rectangle = height of the cylinder

$b = h_1 = 10\text{cm}.$

$V_1 = \pi r^2 h_1 = \frac{22}{7} \times \frac{11}{\pi} \times \frac{11}{\pi} \times 10 = \frac{22}{7} \times \frac{7}{2} \times \frac{7}{2} \times 10 = 385\text{cm}^2$

FOR RECTANGLE 2:

breadth of the rectangle = circumference of circular base of the cylinder

$b = 2\pi r_2 = 10\text{cm}$

$r_2 = \frac{10}{2\pi} = 1.59\text{cm}$

length of the rectangle = height of the cylinder(h_2) $= 22$ cm.

$V_2 = \pi r^2 h_2 = \frac{22}{7} \times 1.59 \times 1.59 \times 22 = 174.8\ \text{cm}^3$

RESULT

Volume of these two cylinders is not same.

LEARNING OUTCOME

Students can easily understand the concept that the volume of the right circular cylinder formed by curving a rectangular sheet along its length is not equal to the volume of the cylinder formed by curving another rectangular sheet of the same dimensions along with its breadth.

ACTIVITY TIME

1. A cylinder is formed by curving a rectangular sheet 22 cm × 20 cm along its length. Another cylinder is formed by curving a squared sheet of side 22 cm along its any side. Compare the volume of two cylinders so formed.

VIVA-VOCE

Question1. If the height of a right circular cylinder is halved and radius of the base is doubled, what effect will it make on the volume of the cylinder?
Answer: The volume will become double the original volume.

Question 2. If the radius of the base of a right circular cylinder is halved, how many times the height should become to keep the volume same?
Answer: 4 times the original height

Question 3. Find the volume of a cylinder for radius 2 cm and height 1 cm.
Answer: $4\ \text{cm}^3$

Question 4. What will be the height of a right circular cylinder if the number of units in its volumeis equal to the number of units in area of its base?
Answer: $h = 1$ unit.
(**Hint:** $\pi r^2 h = \pi r^2$)

Question 5. If the height of a cylinder is twice the radius of its base, then find its volume in termsof height.
Answer: $\frac{\pi}{4}h^3$ cubic units,
where h—height of the cylinder.

MULTIPLE CHOICE QUESTION

Question 1.
If the circumference of the base of a cylinder is 44 cm and height is 10 cm, then the volume of the cylinder is
(a) $1540\ \text{cm}^3$
(b) $1450\ \text{cm}^3$
(c) 1045cm^3
(d) none of these

Question 2.
If the height of a cylinder is four times the radius of its base, then the volume interms of height is
(a) $\frac{\pi}{12}h^3$
(c) $\frac{\pi}{8}h^3$
(b) $\frac{\pi}{16}h^3$
(d) none of these

Question 3.
If the volume of a right circular cylinder is $2\pi r$ cubic units, then find the relation between its radius and height.
(a) $h = 2r$
(b) $h = \frac{2}{r}$
(c) $h = \frac{4}{r}$
(d) none of these

Question 4.
The volume of a cylindrical container is 264 m^3. How many full bags of wheat can be emptied to fill up the container if the space required for wheat in each bag is
(a) 66 bags
(c) 132 bags
(b) 528 bags
(d) none of these

Question 5.
If the circumference of the base of a cylinder is 132 cm and its height is 25 cm, then the volume of the cylinder is
(a) $34650\ \text{cm}^3$
(b) $34605\ \text{cm}^3$
(c) $36405\ \text{cm}^3$
(d) $35406\ \text{cm}^3$

Question 6.
Volume of a cylinder of base radius 2 cm and height 1 cm is
(a) $16.2\ \text{cm}^3$
(b) $12.4\ \text{cm}^3$
(c) $14.2\ \text{cm}^3$
(d) $12.6\ \text{cm}^3$

Question 7.

What will happen to the volume of a cylinder, if its radius is doubled keeping the height same?

(a) two times the original one
(b) half of the original one
(c) four times the original one
(d) none of these

Answer Key

1.(a)	2.(b)	3.(b)	4.(c)	5.(a)	6.(d)	7.(c)

ACTIVITY 22

SURFACE AREA OF A SPHERE

OBJECTIVE

To find the surface area of the sphere with the help of an activity.

MATERIAL REQUIRED

A solid spherical plastic ball, a cylinder with height equal to the diameter of the sphere, thread, cutter, pins, sketch pen etc. (Let radius of sphere be rand height of the cylinder be h)

THEORY

Curved surface area (C.S. A.) of a right circular cylinder = $2\pi r$ (where r =radius of thebase and h = height of the cylinder)

PROCEDURE

1. Divide the spherical plastic ball into two hemispherical portions with the help of a cutter.
2. Fix a pin at the top most point of the hemisphere.
3. Take a roll of thread and wind it closely on the curved surface of the hemisphere completely in the form of a spiral starting with the pin on the surface of the hemisphere
4. Take another roll of thread and wind it completely along the curved surface of the cylinder in the form of a spiral.
5. Unwind the threads from the hemisphere and cylinder.
6. Compare the length of two threads used in wrapping.

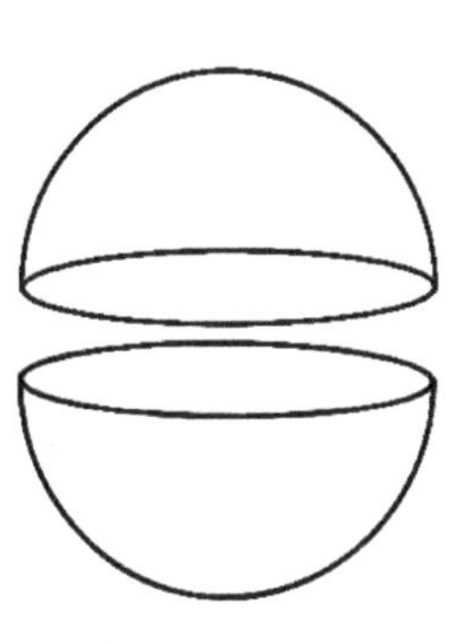

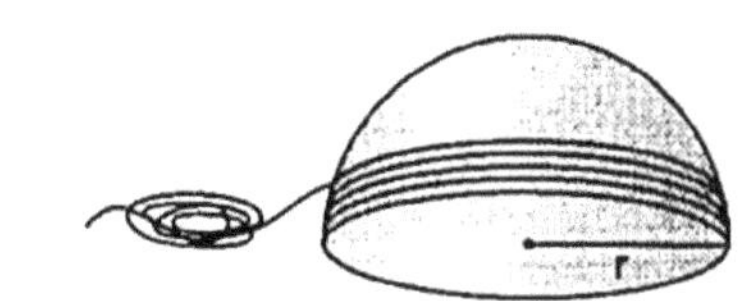

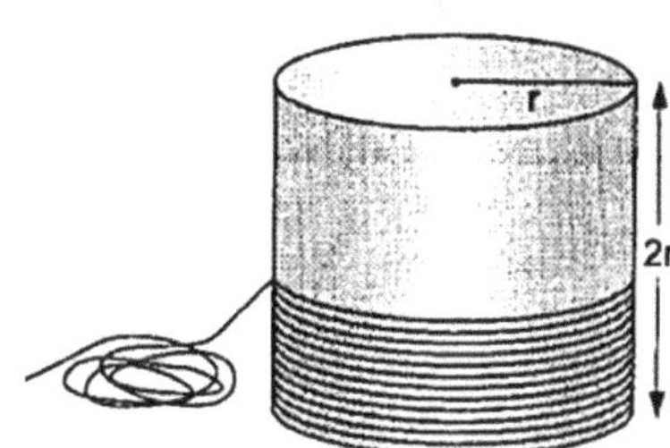

OBSERVATION

1. The length of the thread used to cover the cylinder is two times more than the length of the thread used to cover the hemisphere.
2. Curved surface area of the hemisphere = $\frac{1}{2}$ × curved surface area of the cylinder.

$$= \frac{1}{2} \times 2\pi rh$$

$$= \pi rh$$

$2\pi r^2$ (i.e., $h = 2r$ because the height of the cylinder = diameter of the sphere)

The total surface area of sphere = $2 \times 2\pi r^2$

RESULT

The surface area of a sphere = $4\pi r^2$ (verified experimentally).

LEARNING OUTCOME

Students will derive the formula for the surface area of a sphere through an activity.

ACTIVITY TIME

Let the radii of a sphere and the base of a cylinder be same. Find the ratio of the curved surface area of a sphere to the curved surface area of a cylinder if the height of the cylinder is 2 times its radius.

VIVA-VOCE

Question 1. What is a hemisphere?
Answer: Half of a sphere is called a hemisphere.

Question 2. How many hemispheres make a sphere?
Answer: Two.

Question 3. What is the curved surface area of a hemisphere?
Answer: $2\pi r^2$.

Question 4. What is the curved surface area of a sphere?
Answer: $4\pi r^2$.

Question 5. What is the total surface area of a hemisphere?
Answer: $3\pi r^2$

Question 6. What is the surface area of a sphere of diameter 14 cm?
Answer: 616 cm^2.

Question 7. What is the curved surface area of a sphere of radius 3 cm?'
Answer: $36\pi \text{ cm}^2$.

MULTIPLE CHOICE QUESTION

Question 1.
Surface area of a sphere of diameter 21 cm is
(a) 1386 cm^2
(b) 1368 cm^2
(c) 1683 cm^2
(d) 1863 cm^2

Question 2.
Find the total surface area of a hemisphere of radius 10cm.
(a) 924 cm^2
(b) 492 cm^2
(c) 942 cm^2
(d) none of these

Question 3.
What is the radius of a sphere whose surface area is 154 cm"?
(a) 3.5 cm
(b) 3.3 cm
(c) 5.3 cm
(d) 5.5 cm

Question 4.
The diameter of the moon is approximately one-fourth of the diameter of the earth. Find the ratio of their surface areas.
(a) 1: 16
(b) 16: 1
(c) 1: 4
(d) none of these

Question 5.
A right circular cylinder just encloses a sphere of radius r. Then what is the ratio of the surface area of the sphere to the curved surface area of the cylinder?
(a) $1:1$
(b) $4:1$
(c) $1:4$
(d) none of these

Question 6.
A sphere of radius r has the same volume as that of a cone with a circular base ofradius r. Find the height of the cone.
(a) $2\ r$
(b) $4\ r$
(c) $3\ r$
(d) none of these

Question 7.
What is the surface area of a sphere of diameter 3.5 m?
(a) $38.5m^2$
(b) $35.8m^2$
(c) $53.8m^2$
(d) none of these

Question 8.
If the radii of a sphere and base of a cylinder are same, then find the ratio of the curved surface area of a sphere to the curved surface area of the cylinder if the height of thecylinder is 4 times its radius.
(a) $2:1$
(b) $1:2$
(c) $1:4$
(d) $4:1$

Question 9.
If the surface area of a sphere is 5544 cm^2, then its diameter is
(a) 42 cm
(b) 24 cm
(c) 22 cm
(d) 44 cm

Question10.
The radius of a spherical balloon increases from 7 cm to 14 cm as air is being pumped into it. Find the ratio of surface areas of the balloon in the two cases.
(a) $4:1$
(b) $1:4$
(c) $1:1$
(d) $4:4$

Answer Key

1.(a)	2.(c)	3.(b)	4.(a)	5.(a)	6.(a)	7.(b)	8.(a)	9.(b)	10.(b)

ACTIVITY 23

VOLUME OF A SPHERE

OBJECTIVE
To find the formula for the volume of a sphere with the help of an activity.

MATERIAL REQUIRED
A hollow hemispherical plastic ball, a cylinder with diameter and height both equal tothe diameter of the hemisphere, sand.

THEORY
Volume of a cylinder $= \pi r^2 h$

PROCEDURE
1. Take a hollow hemisphere fill it with sand and empty it into the cylinder. Fig.

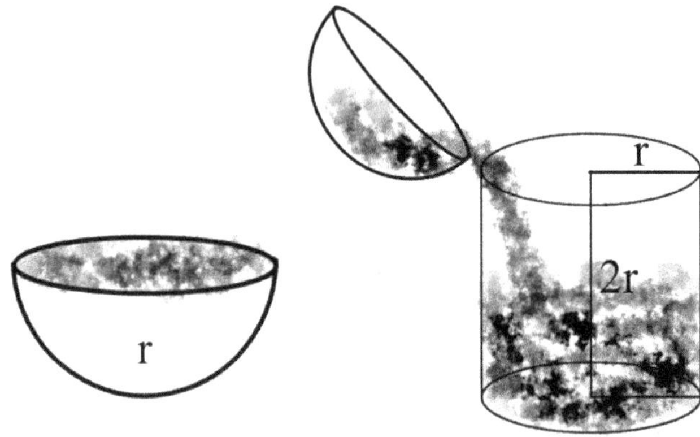

2. Again, fill the hemisphere with sand and empty it into the same cylinder second time. Fig.

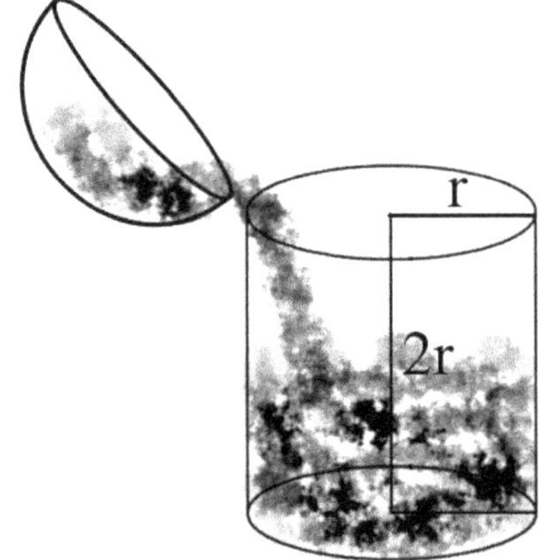

3. Again, fill the hemisphere with sand and empty it into the same cylinder the third time., fig.

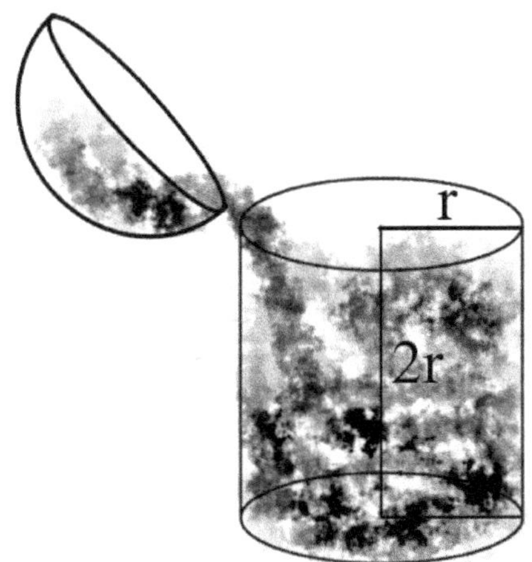

OBSERVATION

Observation

We observe that the cylinder is filled up by pouring sand three times through hemispherical ball.

$\therefore 3x$ Volume of hemisphere = Volume of the cylinder with radius r and height $2r$

$\therefore 3x$ Volume of hemisphere $= \pi r^2(2r) = 2\pi r^3$

$\therefore$ Volume of a hemisphere $= \dfrac{2\pi r^3}{3}$

$\therefore$ Volume of sphere $= 2 \times \dfrac{2\pi r^3}{3} = \dfrac{4\pi r^3}{3}$

RESULT

Volume of a sphere $= \frac{4\pi r^3}{3}$ (verified experimentally).

LEARNING OUTCOME

Students arrive at the formula for the volume of a sphere, and they can relate it with the volume of a cylinder.

Volume of a sphere = volume of a cylinder.

$$= \frac{4\pi r^3}{3} = \pi r^2 h$$

$\therefore h = \frac{4}{3} r$ (if they have same radius and volume)

ACTIVITY TIME

If the radius of the sphere is tripled, then what will be the effect on its volume? Verify it by activity.

VIVA-VOCE

Question 1. What is the formula for volume of a hemisphere?

Answer: $\frac{2\pi r^3}{3}$, where $r =$ radius of hemisphere

Question 2. If the number of square centimetres on the surface of a sphere is equal to thenumber of cubic centimetres in its volume. What is the radius of the sphere?

Answer: 3 cm.

Question 3. What is the volume of a sphere?

Answer: $\frac{4\pi r^3}{3}$, where r is the radius of the sphere

Question 4. Metallic spheres of radii 3 cm, 4 cm and 5 cm respectively are melted to form a single solid sphere. Find the radius of the resulting sphere.

Answer: 6 cm.

Question 5. How many balls each of radius 1 cm can be made from a solid sphere of lead of radius 8 cm?

Answer: 512 balls.

Question 6. What is the ratio of the volume of a cube to that of a sphere which will exactly fitinside the cube?

Answer: $6: \pi$.

Question 7. What is the ratio of the volume of a sphere to that of a cone whose height and radiusof base are same as radius of the sphere?

Answer: 4: 1

Question 8. What is the ratio of the volume of a hemisphere to that of a sphere of same radius?

Answer: 1: 2

MULTIPLE CHOICE QUESTION

Question 1.

What is the ratio of the volume of a cube to that of a sphere which will exactly fitinside the cube?

(a) $6: \pi$

(b) $\pi: 6$

(c) $\pi: 3$

(d) $3: \pi$

Question 2.

The largest sphere is carved out of a cube of side 7 cm. The volume of the sphere is

(a) 179.5 cm^3

(b) 197.5 cm^3

(c) 791.5 cm^3

(d) 971.5 cm^3

Question 5.

Find the volume of a sphere of radius 0.63 m.

(a) 1.05 m^3

(b) 2.05 m^3

(c) 3.05m^3

(d) none of these

Question 3.

If the surface area of a sphere is 616 cm^3, then its volume is

(a) 1473.3 cm^3

(b) 1437.3 cm^3

(c) 1743.3 cm^3

(d) none of these

Question 4.

How many litres of milk can a hemispherical bowl of a diameter of 10.5 cm hold?

(a) 0.309 l

(b) 0.330 l

(c) 0.303 l

(d) 0.003 l

Question 6.

How many lead balls each of 3 cm radius can be made from a sphere of radius 12cm?

(a) 62

(b) 64

(c) 63

(d) 61

Question 7.
A hemispherical bowl has a radius of 3.5 cm. What would be the volume of water it would contain?
(a) $64\ cm^3$
(b) $63\ cm^3$
(c) $62\ cm^3$
(d) none of these

Question 8.
A metallic sphere of diameter 21 cm is melted and recast into a number of smaller cones each of diameter 7 cm and height 3 cm. Find the number of cones so formed.
(a) 162
(b) 126
(c) 612
(d) 621

Question 9.
The diameter of a sphere is 42 cm. It is melted and drawn into a cylindrical wire of a diameter 28 cm. Find the length of the wire.
(a) 63 cm
(b) 61 cm
(c) 64 cm
(d) 60 cm

Question 10.
The diameter of the moon is approximately one-fourth the diameter of the earth. What fraction of the volume of the earth is the volume of the moon?
(a) 1: 64
(b) 64: 1
(c) 1: 1
(d) none of these

Answer Key

1.(a)	2.(a)	3.(b)	4.(c)	5.(a)	6.(b)	7.(d)	8.(b)	9.(a)	10.(a)

PROBABILITY

OBJECTIVE

To set the idea of the probability of an event through a double colour cards experiment.

MATERIAL REQUIRED

Cardboard of size 18 cm × 18 cm, two colour papers say pink and blue, pair of dice,empty box, pair of scissors, sketch pens, fevicol, etc.

THEORY

1. Sample space and event.
2. The total number of possible outcomes.
3. Favourable outcomes.
4. Probability of an event = $\frac{\text{No. of favourable outcomes}}{\text{Total no .of Possible outcome}}$.

PROCEDURE

1. Paste different colour papers, blue and pink on both sides of the board,(such that pink on one side and blue on another side)
2. Divide the board into 36 small, squared cards.
3. Write all 36 possible outcomes obtained by throwing two dice, e.g., for the outcome (4,5), write 4 on the blue side and 5 on the pink side.
4. Cut and put all the cards into a box.
5. Now take out each card one by one without replacement and write the observation in the appropriate column.

OBSERVATION

1. Total number of possible outcomes =
2. Total number of favourable outcomes of sum 2 =
3. Total number of favourable outcomes of sum 3 =
4. Total number of favourable outcomes of sum 4 =
5. Total number of favourable outcomes of sum 5=
6. Total number of favourable outcomes of sum 6 =
7. Total number of favourable outcomes of sum 7 =
8. Total number of favourable outcomes of sum 8 =
9. Total number of favourable outcomes of sum 9 =
10. Total number of favourable outcomes of sum 10 =
11. Total number of favourable outcomes of sum 11 =
12. Total number of favourable outcomes of sum 12 =
13. Total number of favourable outcomes (sum ≥11) =
14. Total number of favourable outcomes (sum >12) =
15. Total number of favourable outcomes (sum < 7) =

Using formula calculates the required Probability of each event. Sample space (when two dice are thrown)

(1,1)	(1,2)	(1,3)	(1,4)	(1,5)	(1,6)
(2,1)	(2,2)	(2,3)	(2,4)	(2,5)	(2,6)
(3,1)	(3,2)	(3,3)	(3,4)	(3,5)	(3,6)
(4,1)	(4,2)	(4,3)	(4,4)	(4,5)	(4,6)
(5,1)	(5,2)	(5,3)	(5,4)	(5,5)	(5,6)
(6,1)	(6,2)	(6,3)	(6,4)	(6,5)	(6,6)

Example: Number of favourable outcomes of the sum of numbers 2=1Total outcomes = 36

∴ The probability of the sum of numbers is 2 $= \frac{1}{36}$

Similarly, find other probabilities for different outcomes of the sum.

RESULT

Probability of an event = $\frac{\text{No. of favourable outcomes}}{\text{Total no .of Possible outcome}}$

LEARNING OUTCOME

The concept of finding the probability of an event is clear through this activity.

ACTIVITY TIME

1. What is the probability of getting the sum of two numbers more than17?
2. Write the sample space, when a coin is tossed 3 times.
3. A game of chance consists of spinning an arrow that comes to rest pointing at one of the numbers 1, 2, 3, 4, 5, 6, 7, 8 as shown in the fig. and these are equally likely outcomes. What is the probability that it will point at

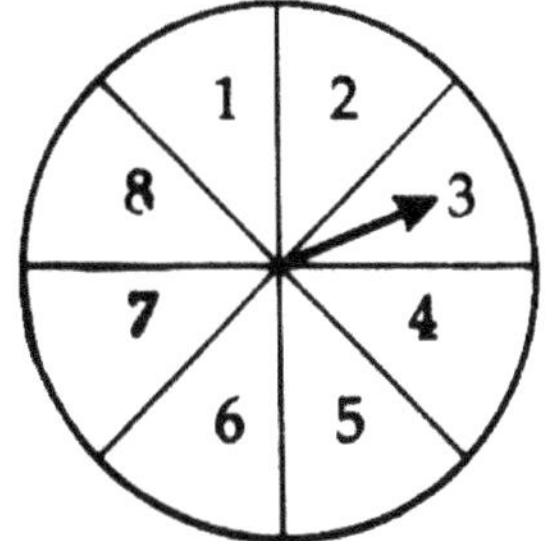

- 3?
- an odd number?
- a number greater than 2?
- a number less than 9?
- a number less than 1?

VIVA-VOCE

Question 1. What is probability?

Answer: The possibility (or possibilities) of occurring or not occurring of an event is called probability.

Probability of an event = $\frac{\text{No. of favourable outcomes}}{\text{Total no .of Possible outcome}}$

Question 2. What is a sample space?
Answer: It is the set of all possible outcomes of a random experiment.

Question 3. What is the probability of an impossible event, sure event respectively?
Answer: Zero, one.

Question 4. A dice is thrown twice. How many elements are possible in sample space?
Answer: 36.

Question 5.
One card is drawn from a well-shuffled deck of 52 cards. What is the probability of aking of red colour?
Answer: $\frac{2}{52} = \frac{1}{26}$

Question 6. If P(E) = 0.05, what is the probability of 'not E'?
Answer: 0.95.

Question 7. A bag contains 3 red and 5 black balls. A ball is drawn at random. What is the probability that the ball is red?
Answer: $\frac{3}{8}$

Question 8. A die is thrown once. What is the probability of getting a prime number?
Answer: $\frac{3}{6} = \frac{1}{2}$

Question 9. What is the sum of the probabilities of all the elementary events of an experiment?
Answer: One

MULTIPLE CHOICE QUESTION

Question 1.
A die is thrown twice. What is the probability that 5 will not come up either?(Hint: meaning is 5 is not coming in the first throw as well as in the second throw).
(a) $\frac{25}{36}$ (c) $\frac{15}{36}$
(b) $\frac{17}{36}$ (d) none of these

Question 2.
17 cards numbered $1,2,3, \ldots 17$ are put in a box and mixed. One person draws a card. Find the probability that the number on the card is prime.
(a) $\frac{15}{17}$ (c) $\frac{8}{17}$
(b) $\frac{7}{17}$ (d) $\frac{9}{17}$

Question 3.
The king, queen and jack of clubs are removed from a pack of 52 cards and then well shuffled. One card is selected from the remaining cards. Find the probability of getting 'The '10' of heart'.
(a) $\frac{1}{49}$ (c) 1049
(b) 949 (d) none of these

Question 4.
A bag contains 5 red and some blue balls. If the probability of drawing a blue ball is double that of a red ball, find the number of blue balls in the bag.
(a) 10
(b) 5
(c) 20
(d) none of these

Question 5.
A coin is tossed three times what is the probability of getting the same result in each trial?
(a) 14
(b) 18
(c) 38
(d) None of these
(**Hint:** TTT or HHH, $\therefore 28=14$)

Question 6.
If P(E)=0.65 then P is $(\bar{E})$
(a) 0.15
(b) 0.30
(c) 0.35
(d) none of these

Question 7.
Which of the following cannot be the event of probability?
(a) $\frac{2}{3}$
(b) -1.5
(c) 15%
(d) 0.7

Question 8.
If probability of 'not E' is 0.98, then P(E) is
(a) 0.5
(b) 0.02
(c) 0.005
(d) 1

Question 9.
In a non-leap year, there are 365 days i.e., 52 weeks and 1 day. Find the probability of getting 53 Sunday.
(a) $\frac{1}{7}$
(b) $\frac{2}{7}$
(c) $\frac{3}{7}$
(d) none of these

Question 10.
Find the probability of getting 53 Mondays in a leap year.
(a) $\frac{1}{7}$
(b) $\frac{2}{7}$
(c) 1
(d) none of these

Answer Key

1.(a)	2.(b)	3.(c)	4.(a)	5.(a)	6.(c)	7.(b)	8.(b)	9.(a)	10.(b)

Experiment No. .... Date. ....

Remarks...................... Teacher's Signature ....

Experiment No. ....

Date. ....

Remarks......................

Teacher's Signature ....

Experiment No. .... Date. ....

Remarks...................... Teacher's Signature ....

Experiment No. ....

Date. ....

Remarks......................

Teacher's Signature ....

Experiment No. ....   Date. ....

Remarks......................   Teacher's Signature ....

Experiment No. ....   Date. ....

Remarks......................   Teacher's Signature ....

Experiment No. ………………… Date. ………………………

Remarks………………… Teacher's Signature ………………………

Experiment No. .... Date. ....

Remarks...................... Teacher's Signature ....

Experiment No. ....

Date. ....

Remarks.....................

Teacher's Signature ....

Experiment No. .... Date. ....

Remarks...................... Teacher's Signature ....

Experiment No. ....

Date. ....

Remarks......................

Teacher's Signature ....

Experiment No. .... Date. ....

Remarks...................... Teacher's Signature ....

Experiment No. ....

Date. ....

Remarks......................

Teacher's Signature ....

Experiment No. .... Date. ....

Remarks...................... Teacher's Signature ....

Experiment No. ....   Date. ....

Remarks......................   Teacher's Signature ....

Experiment No. ....

Date. ....

Remarks......................

Teacher's Signature ....

Experiment No. ....

Date. ....

Remarks......................

Teacher's Signature ....

Experiment No. ....

Date. ....

Remarks......................

Teacher's Signature ....

Experiment No. ....

Date. ....

Remarks......................

Teacher's Signature ....

Experiment No. ....   Date. ....

Remarks......................   Teacher's Signature ....

Experiment No. .... Date. ....

Remarks...................... Teacher's Signature ....

Experiment No. .... Date. ....

Remarks..................... Teacher's Signature ....

Experiment No. ....

Date. ....

Remarks......................

Teacher's Signature ....

Experiment No. ....   Date. ....

Remarks......................   Teacher's Signature ....

Experiment No. .... Date. ....

Remarks...................... Teacher's Signature ....

Experiment No. ....   Date. ....

Remarks......................   Teacher's Signature ....

Experiment No. ....

Date. ....

Remarks......................

Teacher's Signature ....

Experiment No. ....

Date. ....

Remarks......................

Teacher's Signature ....

Experiment No. ....

Date. ....

Remarks......................

Teacher's Signature ....

Experiment No. ....   Date. ....

Remarks......................   Teacher's Signature ....

Experiment No. ....   Date. ....

Remarks......................   Teacher's Signature ....

Experiment No. .... Date. ....

Remarks..................... Teacher's Signature ....

Experiment No. ....   Date. ....

Remarks......................   Teacher's Signature ....

Experiment No. .... Date. ....

Remarks...................... Teacher's Signature ....

Experiment No. ....   Date. ....

Remarks.......................   Teacher's Signature ....

Experiment No. ....

Date. ....

Remarks......................

Teacher's Signature ....

Experiment No. .... Date. ....

Remarks...................... Teacher's Signature ....

Experiment No. .... Date. ....

Remarks........................ Teacher's Signature ....

Experiment No. .... Date. ....

Remarks...................... Teacher's Signature ....

Experiment No. ....

Date. ....

Remarks......................

Teacher's Signature ....

Experiment No. ....   Date. ....

Remarks.....................   Teacher's Signature ....

Experiment No. ....   Date. ....

Remarks......................   Teacher's Signature ....

Experiment No. .... Date. ....

Remarks...................... Teacher's Signature ....

Experiment No. ....

Date. ....

Remarks.....................

Teacher's Signature ....

Experiment No. ....   Date. ....

Remarks......................   Teacher's Signature ....

www.ingramcontent.com/pod-product-compliance
Ingram Content Group UK Ltd.
Pitfield, Milton Keynes, MK11 3LW, UK
UKHW061133310726
14090UKWH00037B/1283

9 789355 563453